The Dustman's Daughter

The Chronicles of a woman's escape from Muslim tradition in France and her story of survival ... to inner peace

Fatima Benzaoui

The Dustman's Daughter
Fatima Benzaoui

This edition Copyright © 2016 by Oxford eBooks Ltd.

www.oxford-ebooks.com
Story Copyright © 2015 by Fatima Benzaoui

The right of the author to be identified as the author of this work
has been asserted in accordance with the
Copyright, Designs and Patents Act 1988.

All rights reserved.
No part of this publication may be reproduced, stored in a retrieval system, or transmitted, in any form or by any means, electronic, mechanical, photocopying, recording or otherwise, without the prior permission of the copyright owners.

ISBN 978-1-910779-24-8 (Paperback)
ISBN 978-1-910779-07-1 (ePUB)
ASIN B0102RDIBI (Kindle)

Introduction

It all started on the 15th August 1983 when finally I decided to take the risk and change my life from a secure and protective family to the wild outside world where, at the time, I believed nothing or no one could be trusted! I was twenty-one years old.

"I opened the car window and felt the fresh air, feeling ever so relieved, happy and thanking the Universe and everyone who came to my rescue in this nearly impossible mission which could have ended in death! It was now the beginning of a new life and I didn't know what was in store for me yet I was trusting."

Chapter 1

Everyone finds himself in the world where he belongs. The essential thing is to have a fixed point from which to check its reality now and then. Always watch and follow nature.

MY FAMILY

I was born into a Muslim family; one of fourteen - I was number nine, (a lucky number in India) and the fourth of five daughters. I was *quite* different. Very early in life, I had a clear vision that my future could be better since I saw my parents, both illiterate, struggle in silence to raise and feed us, all fourteen of us. This had a deep impact on me and hurt me. The only income we had was from my Dad who worked for the Paris town hall as a dustman whilst my Mum kept herself busy getting pregnant, giving birth, looking after new-borns or trying to decide what to feed us all that evening.

Looking back now, I am really impressed with how she successfully managed our home. We never starved, nor were cold, always had a warm bed and there was always food on the stove – especially those delectable thick soups kept warm for us on the *mazhout* (a gas heater with food warmer) during those really cold winter months in France. What a wonderful feeling to come inside after play, freezing cold and slowly slurping this warm thick liquid into our cold little bodies – it was delicious!

My parents, who were cousins, were married in a village called Taghzout, located in the Sahara desert some two hundred kilometres southeast of Algiers. She was 15, he was 31 years old! Muslim religion considers a woman ready for marriage as soon as her periods start, a clear sign that she could now conceive.

The age difference didn't really matter to them and it was completely acceptable to see young beautiful women marrying older men who could offer them a home and look after a family.

In those remote places, it was very common to see marriages

amongst cousins, a way to keep the family close by; although it took no consideration of the possible pregnancy problems caused by in-breeding.

Once married, my parents lived in their home village for a while then moved across the border to Tunisia where my father could have a better chance of getting a well-paid job and raise a family.

Eventually, my father got a good job and managed to earn decent money. They spent ten years of their lives there during which time my Mum gave birth to four children; two sons and two daughters, my eldest brothers and sisters.

At some point during those ten years, my Dad heard rumours that life in France was better, with better job prospects and even better wages. One day after discussing it with my mother, he journeyed alone to Paris by boat and road, leaving my Mum in Tunisia with their four young children.

Luckily we had other members of my family living nearby so she wasn't totally by herself. The idea was that once he settled into a job and got a home in Paris, my Mum would then follow with the children. This eventually happened and she went with one of my uncles who escorted her with her four children and his own family to France by boat.

She never talked at length with me about this amazing journey. For me it was as though a part of her life happened and was forgotten even though she never travelled much more than that later in her life. From what I know, she only ever travelled between France and Algeria by plane to visit family and friends later, once to London to visit me.

My mother used to describe the shanty town called Bidonville in which they first lived as very basic homes with corrugated tin roofs (*"des toits de tolles"*). This was in Nanterre, a suburb in the west of Paris. When it was raining, water got through and made cold winter months even more unbearable.

At that time, my father was earning a regular income and life was actually looking up for them. There, my mother gave birth to two more of my eldest brothers and sisters.

Two years later, my parents were given a two-bedroom

bungalow with a tiny garden in *La Cite Jeanne D'Arc* (Joan of Arc), occupying lucky number 13 for some twenty years. Being quite superstitious, I knew that number 13 was not really a good number, though nothing really dramatic ever happened there which in turn made me question my superstitious beliefs.

I have very fond memories of this place where I was born and grew up. I made my first close friends, began adolescence, became interested in men, got the beginning of my education by going to the nearby primary school – *Ecole du Petit Nanterre* – a short walk *from La Cite Jeanne D'Arc*.

La Cite was composed of twenty-four one and two bedroom bungalows. There was a mix of large families living there from various parts of Algeria, four working class French families and a gypsy family. This is where I spent the next fifteen years, which perhaps were the most important years of my life.

I enjoyed very happy moments there playing with my neighbourhood friends. We lived next door to Jacqueline's family who became one of our best neighbours. She was married to Gugus with four children.

Like most working class families, most likely to forget their financial worries, they drank a lot of alcohol. We would often hear the sound of arguments coming from their house.

The boys of La Cite often harassed their young, good-looking daughter Nenette, as they considered her an easy sexual target, being from a *French* family. The boys knew very well the other, mostly Algerian, girls of La Cite were not to have sex before marriage and didn't even approach them or even if they did, did so with respect, possibly seeing an eventual future wife in her.

Traditionally, a girl born in a Muslim family was supposed to be married whilst still a virgin and had to prove it during the marriage ceremony. This took place during the newlyweds' first night whilst the marriage ceremony was taking place to cover some eventual screams of 'pain'. After intercourse, she has to show blood on her nightie to the waiting guests outside who would then cheer and celebrate even more. This completed a successful marriage celebration. If not, depending on how strict the families were, there were serious consequences for girls who couldn't show blood, traditionally leading to being beheaded by a member of the family in order to save family honour. This threat hung over our heads since when we were little, and the fear of being beheaded prevented us from experimenting with sex before marriage.

As my mother continued to give birth to more of us, we were on a long waiting list at the town hall to get a bigger home, meanwhile we had to manage with a two bedroom home space.

My parents arrived at the bungalow with six children and after fifteen years, we were fourteen children living in this tiny, somewhat homely, warm space. The girls occupied one bedroom; my parents and the newborn at the time used the second bedroom whilst the boys spread out in the lounge sometimes on beds, sometimes on mattresses.

It was from this home that in my small but growing mind, a perception of how my life *should* be, began to shape itself, slowly but surely, day by day, hour by hour.

Before they came to France, my father had heard that it would be easy to get a job in there as they were still rebuilding the country after the Second World War, and more specifically work was needed on the railway lines. At the time, France was encouraging immigrants to come to France for this job and the promise of good wages and a home for their family plus other financial and medical help for their families.

All this was coordinated via the town halls of each suburb. For example, because only my Dad was working, the town hall gave help towards the rent and schooling and a certain amount of money per child until they got to eighteen years of age when it stopped. For my parents, with all their children now, it was quite a substantial amount of money helping them to feed and keep their children warm, as well as educated.

At la Cite, I very often played with my brothers and sisters but we often argued and fought over silly reasons that seemed quite real at the time in our childish brains. I remember the day I fought with my brother Hassan and put his head in the trash bin even though he was taller and stronger than me. In another instance, I broke a plate on his head. There was no fear then and

I felt totally protected by the family unit even though I was so aware that girls were not the favourites in a Muslim family. In our own ways, we were all trying to get attention and affection from our parents but it wasn't so easy because there were so many of us to care for. My parents had to split their affection and no doubt secretly had their favourites too.

In our family, affection was not something shown as openly as in other cultures, I can't remember my parents ever giving us big hugs. By the same token, we never saw them show each other affection either and they were our utmost examples! My Mum though did a little gesture and I am not sure she was even aware of what she was doing was in fact the only when she did it; but when my head was resting in her lap, she would massage my scalp with her fingers using firm pressure. Until today, I find that scalp massage so wonderfully pleasant and relaxing, taking me right back to those moments with my Mum.

Because there were so many of us, at times it was difficult for my Mum to keep an eye on all of us at once or give us equal amounts of affection. In hindsight, I can see how we all had to adopt different ways of attracting our parents' attention to receive their affection.

I only understood what happened to me as a two year old toddler after I was a grown-up; having flashbacks to a time when I was sexually abused my two of my eldest brothers. I found the thought of taking advantage of such an innocent and vulnerable baby so terribly disgusting. Some psychological scars remain with me today sometimes affecting my relationships with men making it harder for me to be close to them to enjoy a pleasant, intimate life. If a man approaches me in an abrupt and brutal way, immediately I take refuge within and completely close myself in not giving him any further chance. That's my survival shield protecting me from potential abuse.

My uncles and their children enriched our family life in Nanterre, in the western suburbs of Paris, especially my uncle's children (who was in fact the only uncle I had in France then on my father's side). This was the same uncle who escorted my Mum to Nanterre, where my father was waiting for her. On my mother's side, I had my Uncle Amar who to this day remains my favourite uncle even though he is not with us anymore. His affection for me greatly disturbed my Dad who hated the protective attention he was giving me.

Uncle Amar lived alone in Nanterre, in a *foyer*, a ten-story building where only immigrant men lived. They worked and sent money back home to their families in Algeria for food and to finish building the family home. This was a big ambition for all of them, even my Dad.

Uncle Amar had six children he loved dearly and missed so much since he had to leave them behind in Algeria. He travelled to see them every summer. His ultimate plan was to go back to be with them when he retired and finish his days with them, which was exactly what happened.

My Uncle Amar was very special to me for many reasons. One of them was a vision he held of me in the future as a university student riding my own scooter and holding a very good job! I loved this positive image as it filled me with so much hope. My Dad, on the other hand, as I found out later, didn't really share this vision at all.

We had regular family visits, my Uncle Amar visiting his sister (my Mum) quite frequently at the end of his working day and my uncle on my father's side with his family. On his way home and when school times allowed, my Uncle Amar often gave me a ride to or from school on his motorbike, a time I totally cherished, making my brothers and sisters jealous as he always picked me as his favourite pillion passenger.

I enjoyed many friendships back then at La Cite but one of them was with my friend Jamila who lived on the next strip of bungalows. Many afternoons at teatime, around 4pm she shared with me her delicious fresh half baguette, full of creamy unsalted butter and to this day when I eat this, my memory takes me right back to those wonderful times with her when we played and laughed together outdoors. We played various games, sometimes with a ball and at suppertime we went back to our respective homes until the next day. I don't remember Jamila being at school with me, she was a couple of years younger so we wouldn't be in the same class together and yet we built a very close friendship. Until today, I wonder how we managed to do this.

Night times at La Cite Jeanne D'Arc strange phenomena seemed to be happening. I remember rumours of a ghost roaming around the skip at the top of our road where all families had to go to empty their bins. Once, we were told that one night one of our neighbour boys called Fouzi, saw the skip lift off the ground! On hearing this, my sisters and I got really scared and nervous every time our parents instructed us to go up there and empty our bins! We did it and ran back so fast that we could be flying. We never saw anything strange.

Some nights, my Dad had to put traps for rats, which found a way of getting inside our house causing disturbances. When he got one at night, he came to wake us up to show us his trophy with great pride. It was disgusting and made us scream. Those rats were such horrible looking creatures. I hid my head under my blanket each time he did this in order not to see the dead animal.

One phenomenon I experienced personally was hearing chains being dragged on the ground just outside our front door. Listening carefully, I could never hear any accompanying footsteps and that intrigued me greatly for so long. Footsteps would have indicated a human or animal dragging those chains. My curiosity quickly grew to the point where I wanted to investigate for myself. At the very young age of ten, I became interested in paranormal activities and shared my experiences with a particular friend of mine at school called Sylvie.

Our toilets were next to the main entrance door and had a little tiny window near the ceiling which slid in and out to keep the place properly aired. A few times, I forced myself to climb up on the toilet seat trying to make myself tall enough to get up to the tiny window to see outside. My idea was to try and peep through to see who or what was dragging those chains. I attempted it many times but was far too scared to see so I gave up. In the back of my mind, I wanted this to remain a mystery because discovering whatever truth was on the other side of the wall could be more disturbing or just as bad, something disappointingly mundane.

Until now, the truth remains a mystery and when I tell my sisters this story, they don't seem to remember which makes me think that keeping this as my little secret made it even more exciting and real for me.

Another strange activity was happening in our family home. When no one was in our kitchen, I would often hear the sound of cooking pans clattering about as if someone was preparing a meal. It was weird; it puzzled me so much for a long time and when I asked my Mum about it, she calmly answered, "It's the angels (*les djins*) making their food – don't disturb them". Even though I didn't understand it, it was a nice explanation to have and the way she said it was very reassuring so I believed her and stopped asking questions even though the sounds continued coming from the kitchen at times. I am not sure my other siblings were also aware of this as I never ever discussed it with them, until today I don't know.

We had a back garden with a concrete floor and very often in the summer time, we left the French doors open for fresh air on those hot summer months. One night, as I was doing the washing up with my back to these doors, I very clearly heard the impact of someone jumping into our garden and landing on their feet, the sound that close and so clear. I totally panicked and ran the other way towards the front of the house where my Mum and close neighbours gathered chatting the night away. I didn't feel like explaining what had just happened and felt protected amongst this group of women, who were completely unaware of what I had just experienced alone out there. I remained stuck in the protection of my Mum's lap and didn't move from there for quite a while.

Whilst living at La Cite, I shared a bedroom with bunk beds with my sisters; all four of us in this room sharing a small space of wardrobe each. I often ended up wearing cast-offs from my older sisters and tried to fit my feet into the tiniest shoes because they looked so gorgeous to me then.

My favourite toy was a tiny doll called Fifi, which I cherished so much because she had beautiful plaited hair, but strangely enough, this doll of mine kept disappearing, never to be seen again. My Dad replaced her for me with a new one but it would disappear again. This happened again and again and it was a total mystery to me. We asked everyone and no one knew. It was so weird, mysterious, and without any valid explanation.

My older sister Hanan often talked about some of the strange dreams she had. For example one night, she saw a big man come after her with an enormous slaughtering knife. It was a horrifying experience for her because sometimes she couldn't even tell if it was a dream or reality. She would wake up drenched in sweat and in a panic.

One summer night I was asleep on my lower bunk bed and the air was very hot so I reached out with my left arm to grab the bar of the bunk bed right above me to give myself some room and air. Suddenly, an enormous hand grabbed my little hand pressing it down against the cold metal bar I was holding. It stayed there and didn't move for what seemed to be an eternity ... time stopped for me. I was so frightened I couldn't even scream, I was paralysed by fear. Who could this be? I couldn't feel a presence or sense any body heat which was ever more mysterious for me. A disembodied hand had me in its terrifying grip and I couldn't do anything. When was it going to stop? I woke up the next day and checked my hand for marks but couldn't find any. Once again, I kept this incident to myself. Until today though, I remember that night so clearly. Perhaps this is the reason I tend to be claustrophobic to this day.

Very early on, my sisters realised I had a special ability to make things happen and that by concentrating really hard on a wish, the wish eventually manifested. I believed this too and experimented with this ability quite a few times very successfully.

They came to me with their wishes and I would just sit there in deep concentration with my eyes closed, helping them realise their desires or at least some of them. I learned this technique from our neighbour Jacqueline who was believed to have psychic powers. I had a lot of fun doing it but it was a lot of work and after a while I felt physically drained, it required an extremely vivid imagination and the ability to see things with one's inner eye in precise detail. I personally used this technique to help me when I wanted a positive outcome, like good grades at school for example. By the time we moved from La Cite, I wasn't using this technique anymore. I had become extremely disillusioned with what I believed.

Our good neighbour Jacqueline, living next door to us, lost her battle with cancer and passed away very quickly which was a shock for all of us. With all I had been sharing with her about paranormal activities, I was convinced after her death, I would have some kind of contact with her, to let me know she was okay and what was over there in the hereafter. Nothing ever happened. Gradually, I began questioning many of my beliefs about the subject and never managed to get any answers. So very slowly, as time went on, I discarded my beliefs, one by one, as I started to think the world I believed in didn't actually exist after all. Later, as I matured, I began a quest to find my place in the Universe and have come to peace with myself ... but more on that later.

Soon after Jacqueline passed away I discovered somewhat abruptly, not only was I very afraid of the dark but also I couldn't *see* much in the dark. I clearly had night vision problems and on top of that I was also short-sighted with a hint of astigmatism. This was confirmed when one day in class, the teacher picked me at random, asking me to read the conjugation of a verb written above the big blackboard. I was sitting at the second row of desks and quickly realised I couldn't read. I sat in silence without being able to say anything. Because I was a good pupil the teacher knew something was wrong.

It was a very embarrassing moment for me and very quickly she sent me for an eye test at our school's medical centre. I was diagnosed as very short-sighted and had to wear thick glasses, at least in class. At home, my parents refused to let me wear them because they thought if I wore them a lot it would weaken my eyesight further.

My sister Farida often teased me about my eyesight and purposefully took me to dark alleys, releasing my hand, and left me there not knowing which way to get out. I had to use my hands to feel the space around so as not to knock my head on the walls. For most children, this was a very funny scene indeed and so it was for Farida, but for me, this was a cruel and traumatising experience indeed but I can laugh about it now.

Often when I wanted to be by myself, I wandered alone behind the houses where each house had an allocated storeroom. I was very interested in plants, and I collected verbena from the only tree behind our home. I dried the leaves which I used to make calming herbal teas for the cold winter months. I wanted to know so much more about plants already and read Maurice Messegue's herbal books. I really enjoyed preparing concoctions and experimenting with different plants that I collected all by myself in the wild greens just behind our home. I loved this connection with nature as I was doing this and especially the silence. I wonder why I never thought of becoming an herbalist!

I often enjoyed spending time reading a book, sitting under the sun seated next to Mokhtar, our beautiful German shepherd with whom we grew up. It was just peculiar that in such a large family, nine brothers and four sisters, I still found solace in being alone and actually found time to do it.

A few months after my thirteenth birthday, my Dad announced that Mokhtar had to be put down; with age he had become blind and had difficulty walking. It was a very sad time for all of us and we all cried, he was so devoted to each one of us, and a part of our family for such a long time.

I remember during those cold winter months when one of us was nominated to go out and give him the food my Mum prepared for him from our leftovers. No one wanted to do it, poor Mokhtar, but my parents didn't let us get away with it and always made sure our dog, like us, was fed properly.

Our play times with my siblings and neighbour friends were so much fun. We played games of volleyball from time to time or chased each other from one end of La Cite to the other before my Mum called us for supper. I really enjoyed challenging my brothers in a game of football, tackling the ball which always got me giggling non-stop. I learned to juggle up to three tennis balls against the wall and very much enjoyed that. One had to concentrate on the balls so hard that you couldn't think of anything else which I found very relaxing.

One day though, as I was playing against my parents' bedroom wall in our garden, my Dad suddenly appeared at the door, still half asleep, confiscated my balls and cut them in half with a knife in front of me. Apparently, the resonance of the balls on the wall disturbed him and he couldn't sleep. All the same, I was very upset but I knew I would soon get new balls again.

My sister Hanan, the second oldest daughter, seemed to be the one nominated to help my Mum in the kitchen and with the newborns who seemed to arrive in our home on a regular basis.

I don't think Hanan was ever happy with her role as surrogate mother, she never complained directly and was rather submissive. All her life, she essentially functioned as a victim and my Mum, picking up on her obvious weakness, constantly ordered her around.

On the 22nd November 1962, it was my turn to arrive in this world. Like most of us, I was born at *l'hôpital de Nanterre*, a short walk from La Cite Jeanne D'Arc and our allocated hospital. I was a healthy baby girl weighing just over two kilos and I was born on a Thursday at 3pm.

I was told later, the name Fatima was the name my older brother Fawzy uttered when he was just over two years old. My Mum liked the sound of the name he said and adopted it for me. Maybe my Mum was getting tired of coming up with all those baby names, and unlike other religions, we hold one name and only our father's surname. However, if there is a death in the family whilst a woman is pregnant, she is expected to name the baby after the person who just passed away, depending of course on the sex of the newborn.

It was always very exciting for me to welcome a new baby into our home and I loved getting to know my youngest sibling. I rushed to the crib at a baby's cry to comfort it before an adult appeared.

All these babies were beautiful without exception, and watching them make faces and waving their arms and legs around was fascinating to me.

I experienced some very touching moments with my Dad, though not frequently enough for me. He worked long hours and was out at six in the morning every day. My Mum woke up with him to prepare his breakfast consisting of fresh coffee with hot milk (*café au lait*) plus toast with butter and honey; a breakfast I very much enjoyed sharing with him on mornings when I was up early, and which I loved having myself whenever possible. Upon his return from work at the end of the day, he reclined on the sofa in our lounge and I came and snuggled up to him with my back towards him. I still find this position brings me such great comfort and a feeling of immense protection and security!

Apparently, my Dad was once a big drinker and often came home after work on his bike totally drunk. I am glad I don't recall those images of my strong father who I absolutely looked up to and admired so much for his strength.

With the financial help of the town hall, my parents sent us away on holidays during our long summer school breaks. I so looked forward to when my Dad gave me a ride to the train station on his motorbike. Those were such beautiful moments especially when I desperately tried to hug his large body into my small arms so I wouldn't fall off. I loved feeling his warmth this way, he was so much bigger than me and I was so small.

One of these holidays took place in the region of St. Hilaire in the southeast region of Charentes in France. There, I learned about nature, animals and I fell in love for the first time with a beautiful boy who I never saw again after I returned back home.

Later, they sent us to spend the summer in Belgium, staying with very caring local families. For me, this was a big turning point in my life as it confirmed to me there was definitely another, better way of living even though I was quite happy being in my family. Little did I know what was just around the corner.

First, I stayed with the Trappeniers who were an extremely kind, caring family of farmers who lived just outside Brussels in the village of Erps Kwerps. Two of their daughters had a major influence on my life, being university students. I looked up to them with great admiration.

There were also three lovely sons there and it was great fun playing together in the barns and the fields chasing each other around like children would. The ice cream van, with its particularly recognizable bell, passed every night at the same time when we were already in bed. We were allowed to step outside in our pyjamas to buy a most delicious ice cream, which we slowly savoured in our beds.

My younger brother Hassan joined me one summer. With this family most likely. My parents felt their honour more protected when a family boy was around me. I had no idea what he was supposed to do and neither did he.

The sweet grandmother of the family was well into her eighties and lived, housebound, next door. Every afternoon at teatime, she sat at an open window peacefully watching us play laughing so loud. At one point, she called us over. When we reached her, she gave us some delicious caramels, which we devoured quickly to get more as we were so greedy. She spoke no French, only Flemish and this was the only way she found to enjoy our company right there near her own home.

In time, my parents changed me to another Belgian family. They were the Lambrechts and lived in the same village of Erps Kwerps, northeast of Brussels in the Flemish province of Brabant. There were only three daughters in this family, my parents evidently felt I was safer with no boys around. These girls were set to become great role models for me as again they were seriously studying, preparing themselves for a bright future.

The father was a businessman, running his own windmill whilst his wife managed the home. It was good for me to see so much love and affection displayed openly in this family. They owned two horses and I got the chance to learn how to ride with them and many other things. I had such a great time spending those few summers with them. They even helped me with some of my schoolwork like mathematics, which they knew was my weakest subject.

When I reached the age of thirteen though and had my first period; my summer holidays to Belgium which I so looked forward to each year cruelly stopped. It was a really sad time for me and I felt something had been taken away from me, considerably shrinking my freedom and suffocating me. I was now considered a woman with a potential danger of losing my virginity and becoming pregnant! This meant loss of family honour and bringing shame and humiliation upon our family.

The time came when my Mum began to want to teach me how to cook and look after a home. I was a very studious pupil at school but didn't show any interest in domestic chores. My father really didn't pay any attention to my studies; he was more interested in my brothers' studies and I saw him get into such a rage when they refused to do their homework; but it was all in vain.

As for me, now that I had seen how other people lived, particularly the Belgian families, I began dreaming of a totally different life but at this stage, I had no other option but to go with the flow and accept the family I was born into.

Every year, we observed Ramadhan, the Muslim fasting month, during which time we refrained from eating and drinking from sunrise to sunset. It is a time when Muslims ask for forgiveness from past sins and purify themselves, teaching patience, modesty, and spirituality. A good Muslim follows this ritual once a year, praying five times a day, not eating pork, not drinking alcohol, nor getting angry.

At that time, I was so keen to please my Dad, I started praying and learning Arabic at school. Needless to say, my Dad was so impressed with me which unconsciously was what I wanted, wishing him to recognise me for who I was.

We were still living in La Cite Jeanne D'Arc when it was time for my Dad to go to Mecca and become a *Hadj*. A Hadj is a person who has fulfilled the fifth pillar of Islam through a pilgrimage to the Kaaba in Mecca, Saudi Arabia during the month of Dhu al-Hijja (the twelfth and final month of the Islamic calendar). This must be carried out at least once in a Muslim's lifetime to demonstrate solidarity with the Muslim people and their submission to Allah (God) and cleanse themselves from all their sins in the hope to go to paradise in their afterlife. For a Muslim, the Hadj is the ultimate act of worship.

The Kaaba is a cube-shaped building in Mecca and is the most sacred site in Islam. The Qur'an states that Abraham and his son Ishmael constructed the Kaaba, after Ishmael had settled in Arabia. The building has a mosque built around it, the Masjid al-Haram. All Muslims around the world face the Kaaba during prayers no matter where they are in the world.

When he returned from Mecca (and as per the tradition), everyone including our neighbours gave him such a wonderful welcome home party. In anticipation of his arrival, we purchased a sheep, which we kept in our garden for a few days pending his arrival. Upon his return, my Dad, with the help of a large butcher knife, cut its neck right on the concrete floor of our back garden and in front of all of us. Lots of blood poured out and very soon the sheep stopped moving. This was a normal scene for us because every year to celebrate the end of Ramadhan, a sheep is sacrificed and its meat used to prepare a celebration feast with couscous.

The now dead sheep was then cut open and all the internal edible pieces removed, cleaned, and grilled to be eaten almost immediately. Eyes, brain, and heart were part of this feast too. My Mum, with helpers, prepared couscous, the North African dish made by rolling and shaping moistened semolina wheat and then coating them with finely ground wheat flour. Couscous was served with a thick tomato sauce with cut vegetables and a serving of meat from the freshly cooked sheep.

All guests ate a generous portion of this delicious meal and a larger amount was sent to the local Mosque as part of the giving ritual to thank Allah for a safe return from Mecca.

Shortly after my Dad's return from Mecca, my Mum became pregnant one final time. She was forty-nine years old and gave birth to our youngest brother.

Two years later, the commune of Nanterre informed us that La Cite Jeanne D'Arc was going to be demolished to make space for luxury townhouses and we needed to move out. Eventually, the town hall gave us a three bedroom flat in a high-rise opposite the hospital de Nanterre where almost all of us children were born and just a short walk from La Cite. One by one, we saw our lovely neighbours move away, taking with them the fondest memories of our life at La Cite. All of the families were given flats wherever they were available within the commune of Nanterre and so we were all separated. It was sad every time a family moved out but it was a positive move as we were now going to live in more comfortable homes without the risk of flood.

Floods were a regular occurrence at La Cite because the storm sewers never seemed to function properly. After a hard rain, our homes were inundated with smelly sewage water. Many a time, we had to lift all our belongings off the floor onto a higher surface to protect them from damage and my Mum sang a song to Allah to stop the rain – which continued pouring until it was ready to stop naturally.

When floods happened, I sat there in a daze wondering whether this was the end of the world and whether we were all going to die. My Mum would quickly re-assure me that the rain and water would go, and eventually it always did. We were one of the last families to leave La Cite, perhaps because we were the largest and not so easy to accommodate.

When both our next door neighbours finally moved out and La Cite felt so empty, I began to hear strange sounds coming from across the walls at night. It usually sounded like the shrieks of a baby. It was so scary I couldn't get to sleep after that. Was it the powerful spirit of Joan of Arc coming through to us or to me this time? I often wondered why La Cite was named after her, this young peasant girl who claimed divine guidance and led the French army to several important victories.

She was captured and burned at the stake in 1431 when she was only nineteen years old. Twenty five years later, she was found innocent and was eventually canonised in 1920, 489 years after her death. I never knew the origin of the scary noise and once again, I don't remember sharing this mystery with any of my siblings.

Having waited longer than other families to get our new home, my Dad decided to destroy the wall from the adjacent vacant property to make more room for us. It was great fun to have a bigger home for a little while and be able to spread our things out for a change.

Finally, our turn came to move out and we did so sadly and peacefully, looking forward to a new beginning. I was sixteen years old with a clear vision of my future or at least what it should be like. We settled in our new flat very quickly but it was very unsettling for me, at first not to feel the contact of the earth under my feet now that we were on the third floor.

We didn't have a garden there but we had a large west facing balcony which was great. The town hall helped families like ours by giving them affordable rental accommodation. One of my Dad's precious dreams was to own his own home one day, and even though he made an offer on a few properties in his lifetime, it somehow always fell through. It was painful to see sadness on his face when this happened. I so wanted to be able to help and wondered if I could access my manifestation power for him but sadly, even this didn't work and nothing happened.

I was allocated one of the bedrooms shared with Farida but for an unknown reason, I decided rather than sharing a double bed with her (which I didn't feel comfortable doing), I slept on a mattress on the floor instead. I pulled out the mattress from under her bed every night and pushed it back in the morning. I was in so much need of my own space at this stage. My clothes were kept in a wardrobe in the corridor away from her bedroom. I had a feeling of not being completely settled there and was just passing by.

Finally, I was able to use the next bedroom when my brother Sabir moved out to go and live with his partner Martine. The flat was still a bit small for all of us but we managed as usual and I never heard my parents complain, in fact they were rather happy there would be no more flooding. From this place and without knowing at the time, I was moving steadily and clearly towards my future.

Chapter 2

> *All is within yourself. Know your most inward self and look for what corresponds with it in nature.*

THE SUITOR FROM ALGERIA

My Mum took me to Algeria with her as a toddler so I was only five months old when I took my first flight although I don't remember the experience. It must have been quite painful for my little ears, a common phenomenon for infants with air pressure changes during flights.

She took me with her again as an adolescent of fifteen years of age to visit the family and hopefully find a suitable future husband. My Mum's mission was to secure the future of all her five daughters, this way protecting the family honour. Her primary concern wasn't for our happiness; rather this man was able to take on the job of taking care of the family.

So, during those holidays in Algeria, I was introduced to family and neighbours as a potential spouse for their sons. Indeed, they did love me there because even though I didn't feel particularly pretty at the time, my skin tone was lighter than the other girls. Light skin symbolised cleanliness, innocence and purity which was highly sought after – although I didn't possess the large round hips that would have completed the picture and put me on the beauty list.

I was introduced to one of my first cousins. This boy, who was two years older than I, was reasonably good looking and I liked him as my cousin. At first, we got on really well and played games with stones in the hot sand of the Sahara desert on very hot afternoons, when everyone else was inside having a siesta. Then, I started to realise that not only did he just like me but was also looking at me as a potential future wife.

At that point, it was just fine because deep inside, I didn't understand the implications of what was happening. I didn't say anything and ignored his long stares when he was observing me from a little distance. The holidays came to an end and we left on good terms as good friends and family members.

Alongside an oasis, grew a grove of date palms that my father inherited. They produced dates each year, eaten by the family during the month of Ramadan; when accompanied by a glass of fresh milk they served to break the fast at the end of the day.

Arriving in Algiers from Paris, one of my uncles on my Mother's side came and waited for us at the airport, taking us to his flat in Bab El Oued in central Algiers. Ten people lived in this small, two bedroom flat. Still, he always comfortably accommodated my Mum and whoever was travelling with her, as she couldn't travel by herself.

It was nice getting to know my cousins in Algiers and observe how they lived and functioned at home. The girls always seemed to be inside to help whilst the boys were outside playing - nothing unusual there.

At that time, seventy percent of the population of thirty-five million were under the age of twenty. The boys were mostly found roaming the streets either having dropped out of school early or unable to find jobs. They were dark or blond haired with dark, green or blue eyes. It was fascinating to see such varied beauty, presumably the result of French colonisation of Algeria.

Algiers was a fun place to visit but of course, most of our time was spent visiting members of our family rather than sightseeing, an activity my family was not particularly interested in.

To travel south to my parents' village of Taghzout, we took either an overnight bus or a short flight to the nearest airport of Guemar.

Taghzout, my parents' birthplace is a small village located four hundred miles southeast of Algeria at the Tunisian border, right in the desert. I loved the journey by overnight bus especially when I was awakened at sunrise by the beautiful views of sand dunes all around us, which truly was a magnificent view of this peaceful landscape. On the other hand, the Fokker aircraft we would sometimes take was much faster but with so much air turbulence it was sickening most times.

My eldest brother, Boubaker, was married to a cousin there in the village; he would come to pick us up and take us to our parents' house which he now used as his own family home.

He cared for the place and lived there with his wife Sakina and their seven children. The home had four bedrooms, a kitchen and a lounge; all built as separate rooms around a square courtyard, the usual layout of desert homes.

The kitchen was very basic with a gas stove on the ground, a fridge and shelves to store pots and pans. The shower was just a cubicle in which we had to bring a bucket of heated water and a plastic jug to pour water over ourselves to rinse the soap off our bodies. The toilets were squat toilets with only water to wash ourselves using our left hand - there was no toilet paper. For those Muslims who were praying, this was a compulsory cleansing routine five times a day.

Mornings, we awakened at sunrise around six and my sister-in-law served us hard-boiled eggs and freshly brewed coffee. The day was then filled with visits from members of our family or my Mum and I went to them for lunch or dinner.

To go out in the village, my brother ordered us to wear the veil. My Mum was used to wearing it but I was always rebelling against this piece of fabric which covered my body and face and which I found so impractical. I had to wear it though or else I wasn't going out. The veil constantly kept falling off my face. As soon as it was dark though and my Mum and I walked back to our home, I just let it drop off my face onto my waist until we reached home. She pretended not to have seen anything.

Whilst on holidays, my Mum also went to pay a visit to the cemetery where her parents and members of her family were buried. In fact, for us living overseas, when our turn for death came, our bodies would be flown back to the village and be buried there next to our grandparents and family – our final destination is in the desert. Both my parents and my younger brother Hassan are resting in peace there now.

During those holidays, I loved to go and spend time with my grandfather, my Mum's Dad. He lived on my uncle's farmland by himself, my grandmother having passed away many years ago whilst giving birth to my youngest uncle. Sadly, I never got the chance to meet her but she met me when my Mum took me with her as a baby. During the hot afternoons, my grandfather kindly invited me to come and see him after his siesta and prepared the most delicious mint tea using fresh mint leaves from the garden. He lived in a single room where he had a sleeping area and a little kitchen.

How I loved sitting quietly there with him. His energy was beautifully calming and his deep wisdom was expressed through his eyes that had now almost turned blue.

He limped a little from an accident he had eight years previously. One morning, a car hit his horse and cart while he was on his way to market where he sold vegetables he grew on his land.

He was the only grandparent with whom I felt a real connection at a spiritual level. Sadly, we couldn't talk much. I knew only a little Arabic and he could not speak a word of French. Although our family in Algiers spoke Arabic and French, in the village they only spoke Arabic.

It was the same with my parents living in France, resisted speaking fluent French in an unconscious attempt to retain their identity. It was very difficult for all of us to interact with them at a deeper level. Sometimes, I found this a bit frustrating and later on, I decided to learn Arabic to better my contact with them.

My mother once attempted to take French classes organised locally but she quickly gave up for lack of time having such a large family to look after. My Dad managed well enough with French because he had to with his job.

One year after my last holiday to Algeria, I learned from my Mum that my first cousin and his Mum were coming to visit us in France, officially to make a marriage proposal to me. It was only then that I started to panic, realising what their visit meant. As an adolescent growing up in France, a lot had happened in my life by then. I saw my life in a totally different way from the one my Mum had in mind: get married, have babies, and run the home which meant cooking, cleaning and in this case, I would even have to move to Algiers because he had no plans to live in France. What was I to do now?

I felt so alone. My parents really were excited about this news because for them, marrying their daughters off whilst virgins meant they had accomplished their mission successfully. I spent many nights thinking about how I didn't want the life they offered me.

I was nearly seventeen years old and I wanted to study, to go to University, to have a career, a good job, a house and a lifestyle where I could travel, keep fit and have hobbies I loved doing like dancing! To get myself out of this situation, I came up with a strategy to put my suitor and his mother completely off me.

With the little information I had about life in Algeria, I figured out it would be far more dangerous for me to marry him and move to Algeria because there was no way I could get back to France by myself. It also would be difficult to get a divorce and a woman travelling by herself in an airport always looked suspicious to authorities there. The only option I had was to show them not only I wasn't the attractive girl they thought I was but also I couldn't manage in the kitchen either. When they arrived and everyone around me was getting excited except me, I wore ragged long Arabic dresses which we normally wore while doing household chores.

My hair was tied back and wrapped in an old scarf and I decided to wear my glasses all the time. I was heavily shortsighted and the lenses were thick enough to put anyone off. I started to play awkward in the kitchen by overcooking vegetables and burning dishes on purpose!

Of course my mother wasn't very pleased, seeing that what I was doing was not my normal behaviour and she well knew I wasn't happy with the situation. My strategy worked. After a few days, my potential future mother-in-law became really unhappy with me and started to throw me some ugly looks. They stayed with us for a whole month, but for me it felt like a year and I was so relieved the day they announced they were leaving. They left, angry and disillusioned, realising I was not interested in their proposal and couldn't possibly suit or fit the lifestyle they had in mind for me in Algeria.

Good. It was my turn to be happy, I was so relieved. I achieved my objective and now I could go on and continue with my life and my studies, something I was really keen on doing but I didn't know how many obstacles lay before me. I threw myself into my studies, spending time on my own in my bedroom.

As time went on, I realised my Dad despised seeing books scattered around me on the bed when I was studying and on many occasions he often threatened to burn them. He used all sorts of insulting words when he referred to me like, "the blind one" or, "the dumb one". I thought it was strange that he demonstrated so much hatred towards me because I had chosen a different way of life from the one he expected me to have. Like all good Muslim fathers, he wanted me to be the ideal Muslim girl, practising religion, getting married to a good man, and raising a family. After a short spell at praying, I now gave it up and he so resented me for that.

My education became such an important part of my life and I was determined to pass my Baccalaureat (equivalent to A levels) even though no one else in my family had gone that far with their studies. Even then, Farida one of my older sisters kept discouraging me and repeating it was an unnecessary effort for my future. What a short-sighted statement that was. Instead of giving up, I threw myself even more into my books with no support whatsoever from my family. I was determined to succeed.

I quickly worked out that my Dad, anytime now, would find an excuse to stop my schooling especially since all girls in my family were expected to do their share of house chores. To avoid this reaction, I woke up at 6 A.M. every day to do my chores doing whatever was necessary so he couldn't come up with an excuse. For a few years, I lived with this permanent threat hanging over my head and sometimes I got tired but kept going, with the bigger picture firmly in my sights.

The other reason he could find an excuse to stop me from

going to school was that he couldn't afford to pay for my books, so knowing this, I babysat in secret so I could buy them myself. I also managed successfully to apply for a grant, but my Mum took the bulk of it to buy food and clothes leaving me with very little. Luckily, I was one of those brilliant pupils who attracted the attention of good teachers.

I got very close to my English teacher at Le Lycee Joliot Curie, Mme Vecchini, who contributed towards my books as she could see a potential in me and how determined I was to get a proper education. I will never forget this special person in my life along with a couple more teachers who gave me so much moral support to go on with my studies and get an education so I could better my life. They simply believed in me, it felt good and so empowering.

Chapter 3

By knowing, one reaches belief.
By doing, one gains conviction.
When you know, dare.

EDUCATION

L'Ecole Maternelle du Petit Nanterre (Nursery school)
I really loved this school, my first one. I was three years old and it was my first contact with the world of education, one I enjoyed and which played a big role in my life.

The Maternelle was right next door to the Primary School (*L'Ecole Primaire*) where I went next. At the Nursery, we played games through which we could learn about numbers and colours and then had a long siesta in the afternoons when our teacher drew those navy blue curtains. It used to scare me as the classroom became suddenly really dark. Usually, it was my sister Farida who brought me and picked me up again as she went to the Primary School next door.

My parents clearly trusted the girls more with such responsibilities rather than ask the boys who were expected to be out and about playing with their friends and were a bit unreliable.

I remember arriving early when the Nursery School was still closed and my sister lifted me up and sat me on the high stone steps, which made my bottom feel freezing cold. We just sat there, outside the main entrance door waiting for the door to open.

The school was about fifteen minutes' walk from our home so once washed, dressed, fed and ready to go, we walked together to school passing by some derelict terrain. One morning, we heard a rumour that a newborn baby was found dead in a cardboard box in the rubble. Although we didn't have the courage to go and see for ourselves, I could only imagine a tiny pink motionless body - it was not a pleasant thought. For a while, it put me off eating any kind of meat especially chicken, which my Mum bought live from the market which my Dad would kill using a knife in front of our house. Killing in this way made the meat Halal, the only meat Muslims were allowed to eat.

It was so funny, sometimes he missed a part of the neck and a headless chicken got back on its feet and started to run around until it finally died. For little children, it was hilarious to see and we ran away screaming.

All children spent three years at the Nursery School before moving on to the Primary School next door.

L'Ecole du Petit Nanterre (Primary School)

I was six years old and ready to go to Primary School where all children spent six years of their lives before moving on to College. I felt really proud to enter a bigger school now and was looking forward to more learning. I made this lovely friend in class named Gisele and we often walked back home together. She lived a little way past La Cite Jeanne D'Arc and sometimes I would visit her at her home or she would come to mine. Somehow, my parents didn't mind this although they were always a bit nervous about me mixing with French people for fear that they would turn me away from our Muslim way.

At times, my actions were a little confusing for my parents; especially the time when I had decided to start praying daily. Although this delighted them, it was only my way of gaining the attention and respect of my dad that I so craved.

Compared to my siblings, I very much enjoyed studying so after each day at school, I went home and comfortably settled on the only sofa in our lounge with a stool in front of me as my table conscientiously doing my homework.

I was very aware none of my brothers did any homework after school and I remember my Dad shouting at them, instructing them to do so and only then could they go out and play. What a waste of energy. It was obvious neither my brothers nor my sisters were interested in school or ever would be. In retrospect,

I wonder why my example alone was not enough inspiration for them. Who did I think I was? From where on Earth did I ever get my role model?

For sure, it wasn't my family; it wasn't even a school friend or a teacher at that time, it was more like some unexplained urge coming from within showing me the way.

I so wanted to impress my Dad and would do anything to get his good attention, becoming the perfect example until that day in the future when I would stop praying. We all fasted once a year for Ramadhan but instead of doing it for religious reasons I was using it as a detox diet to cleanse my body from all the deliciously greasy food we ate regularly at home and lost a bit of weight in the process.

At the time, I was trying to show my Dad how good I was as I could see him struggling, pushing my brothers to study and when he got angry with them, he would hit them so hard until once, my family had to intervene to stop him from seriously harming one of them. He had this frightening rage in him that expressed itself when something touched him so deeply. Like all fathers, he wanted his boys to do very well in school so they could have a better future. Compared to others left in Algeria, he thought they had a really good chance in France to achieve this goal.

In a way, he was projecting his own dreams onto his boys and got frustrated when he realised they were not going anywhere. It was during that time, to try and save a couple of them he decided to send two, Fawzy and Abdelkrim to a boarding school. He wanted them to be immersed in a studious environment with no distractions and learn a profession. Fawzy did very well for himself, becoming a carpenter and going on to become a successful and respected professional in his industry. Abdelkrim, on the other hand, came out with a career, which he never properly put to use in his life.

I have really fond memories of my time at Primary School but it was during that time I realised I wasn't very good at mathematics and had to retake a class; I wasn't pleased with that at all. I made it through though and I was ready to leave

Primary School to go on to College which was a bus ride away. I wasn't sure my parents would let me go because taking the bus was an extra expense for them.

Le College Andre Doucet

I was twelve years old and it was the first time I took the bus by myself, without a parent or siblings around. The journey was short and easy and I used to join a girlfriend from La Cite at the bus stop. We chatted and laughed until we reached college. It was great fun taking the bus and seeing adults go to work, giving me an insight into what it might be like to work in an office one day.

My weak mathematics skill confirmed itself at College and instead, I decided to push more in the subjects I was good at; namely languages. I started with English classes then moved on to Arabic and later on at the *Lycee* (High School), I added Spanish to my repertoire of languages with one year of Latin in between. I was really enjoying the language classes and the fact I liked the teachers helped tremendously to make the classes interesting and pleasant. I strongly believed that teachers can either make you like or hate a subject, they have so much power and yet not all are good at passing on the love of the subject they teach.

I was totally ready for College now preparing for the equivalent of O Levels (BEPC), which then would take me onto High School. I needed a grant so desperately since my parents couldn't afford to pay for the books I was going to need. I was so happy when I finally succeeded to get a government grant, which wasn't much, but it was of great help.

Every day of the week now, I took the bus to college, a big thing for my parents, with me being only thirteen years old.

There, I slowly became aware of how other wealthy French students were leading such different lives to mine. I dreamed I could have that too one day especially when one of the girls arrived every morning wearing the *Amazone* Eau de Cologne from Hermes, a perfume I loved then. She was beautiful, intelligent, kind and many nights, I wished that I could be in her shoes and tried to imagine what her life must be like.

One day, out of pure kindness or perhaps even pity, she filled a small bottle of this perfume for me to use since every time she wore it I couldn't help but make a compliment to her. I was just so thrilled to smell as good as she did, and for a few minutes I was in her shoes, living her life.

I was going through adolescence and made quite a few friends at college, male and female, fallen in and out of love with boys though that was mostly platonic love as nothing more than kissing could ever happen because of our strong tradition. It was all happening in my head and I enjoyed daydreaming and imagining myself in a romantic love story which was a forbidden world for me right then.

The first Asian person I met in my life was my mathematics teacher called Mr Trantdang. Even though he was an excellent teacher I was still not good at mathematics and I soon realized I never would be. I enjoyed his class though and I was fascinated by his unusual facial features. I had only seen Asians on television and never so close.

I made close friendships during that time, though nobody that I would ever call a *best* friend. I lost contact with most of them over time; the only way to stay in touch with them was via letters or telephone, the latter we didn't have at La Cite. I often wondered what had become of them and whether they were happy with their lives.

My classmates often commented how seriously I was taking my studies and teased me about it. They tried to make me sing whilst we were waiting for our teacher in front of the classroom. It was then I realised I was so different but didn't know why. I wanted to succeed so much and have a good future and actually enjoyed learning new things. But I overlooked they also wanted to succeed, though doing it a different way, and perhaps a more relaxed way. I was doing it the only way I knew then.

My femininity started to show; my breasts were developing and my periods had started. Luckily, the latter happened at home and although I was expecting their arrival, I went directly to ask my sister Farida about what to do next because my Mum was not expected to teach us those things. In the world I grew up in, we learned from one another.

It was strange though because when my Mum heard that I started to have periods from my sisters, she suddenly started to look at me differently almost like a potential danger. After all, now I could have sex and get pregnant. She became anxious about me, for this responsibility totally resided on her shoulders alone and should anything like this happen, my Dad would blame her.

When she stopped my holidays to Belgium I remained at home helping and learning in the kitchen to make couscous and other delicious dishes she prepared daily for us. I had no interest in this at the time but I had no other option or so I thought then.

At the same time I stopped praying, my Dad was not happy with this and decided to ignore me for a while. I continued studying more and more and was getting better and better grades. Now the life I imagined having was becoming clearer in my inner eye. We were never allowed to go on holidays alone or with friends and we rarely went on holidays as a family to Algeria for example, there were just too many of us!

My summers were mostly spent in Nanterre and later on, my sister Farida nicknamed it 'Nanterre Plage' as she managed a suntan by simply exposing herself to sunshine on our balcony. Our time was mainly spent helping with household chores, spring cleaning, and preparing afternoon teas for family and visiting friends. At times it was so boring, with me dreaming of so many interesting activities I could be doing like going to the museum, to the park, or even exploring a new place.

I learned to play the flute at College and enjoyed reading classical music. One day, our music teacher fainted, collapsing on the classroom floor right in front of all of us. I remember being completely shaken by this incident and when I reached home and told my Mum, she put me straight to bed as she could see I was in total shock. For me, this was the realisation of the fragility of life. I don't even know what happened to our teacher, we never saw her again at College and she was soon replaced by someone else.

One day, whilst I was playing outside at La Cite, running, I collided with another kid running in the other direction, seriously injuring my ankle. In tremendous pain, I limped all the way back home. When my Mum saw me, she immediately put my foot in hot water, massaging it. It was then I discovered my inability to cope with this kind of close attention and felt like running away because it made me feel so claustrophobic. Even though she was upset with me, she still cared for me with so much love and until today I am so grateful to her for showing me this way of being.

Later on, I experienced a similar situation when we lived in the high rise. Whilst I was doing some chores on our balcony, I accidentally cut the index finger of my left hand with a broken mirror placed there waiting to be discarded. My finger starting to bleed heavily, so I used pieces of cotton cloth to stop the blood but without success; it just kept gushing out. After a good hour of losing blood, it finally stopped and I was relieved because I began to feel unwell and weak. No one noticed the bandage and I never mentioned the incident. I still have a scar on that finger. I just wanted to avoid any attention of the caring kind because I knew I wouldn't feel comfortable with it so I dealt with it quietly, in silence and it worked.

In another instance one winter, I ran a very high fever and my Mum of course, insisted on looking after me, and put me to bed and gave me some medicine and hot soup to drink. I remember my attempts at trying to reassure her I was okay so she would leave me alone. Again, felt suffocated receiving so much care and attention. She was the sweetest Mum and I loved her very much yet blocked myself from her love because of my own feelings of claustrophobia or was it to do with my discomfort around closeness?

One day, I came across a place in the borough next to ours where I could take Arabic classes and decided to join their Saturday morning classes. It is strange how even then I was already so self-motivated. I don't remember needing encouragement from my parents to go to those classes. In fact, I tried to convince my younger brothers to join as well. I started to learn Arabic there and really enjoyed the classes. Of course, my brothers started with me but quickly gave up as they were simply not interested. This class was helping me a lot at college where I was also taking Arabic as my second language after English and enjoyed both classes very much. For me this was like expanding my horizons farther than France and I found this simply fascinating.

My Arabic teacher was a very pleasant French man and found him to be such a fascinating person. He had spent quite some years in Algeria and was even involved in the war of independence from France in 1962, my birth year, supporting the Algerians!

I had such a vivid imagination and my mind very often went into a daydream where I visualised I had a magic protecting energy coming to my aid every time I got in trouble in my life. This energy was a giant so much stronger than I and I felt so powerfully protected by him. I just had to call his name, 'Genie' and he would appear. That was so reassuring even though I always looked at my Dad as a strong and powerful man but this genie was mine and mine only and more importantly he understood me.

After four years at the college, we had an exam to pass, the BEPC to qualify for High School. By the time my turn came to pass the test, the government changed the rule and if we had enough good grades throughout the year, the test was waived. Those who didn't pass with their grades were sent to a professional training school where they could learn a profession within two years and get a job. With my good grades, not only did I get the BEPC waived but I also was admitted to High School. The chosen one was *Le Lycee Joliot Curie* named after the Nobel prize winning daughter of Madame Curie who followed in her mother's footsteps, researching radioactive chemistry.

I was so deeply thrilled my efforts were paying off so far. This was about the time we moved from La Cite to our flat in the high rise building where my life was to change forever.

Le Lycee Joliot Curie (High school)

I was sixteen years old and was more than pleased to enter High School preparing for the "big B", the Baccalaureat (equivalent to A levels) in three years. It was my dream, I had been waiting for this all these years. So far, all my desires were going according to plan even though by now, threats of not allowing me to continue my education were growing stronger from my Dad. I was determined to pass my A levels and studied really hard. I made some interesting friends during that time too. One of them became my best friend, her name was Zara and we shared some wonderful and intense growing times together.

I was rather impressed with the fact that even though Zahra was born in Morocco, she managed to brush up her French to such a good level in no time and was able to join the French school system without problem. Unfortunately, I was going to lose sight of most of the lovely friends I made at Le Lycee later on but didn't know it then.

We could talk life philosophy for hours and hours as if able to resolve the world's problems. Of course, we never succeeded, we were such amateur philosophers!

We shared our love stories and missed classes to go for coffee or into Paris for a walk. I was so amazed at Zahra, the way she looked after herself and the way she looked so much like a woman at such a young age, she was beautiful and a very deep thinker and I loved her very much.

We kept a communal diary where we wrote quotes from famous philosophers and writers. Mature men so loved and cherished her. Somehow she seemed to attract older men, perhaps because of her maturity and her feminine looks. It always amazed me how she could manage to find time to go out, and always come up with a good story her Mum completely believed.

I often went to her home in Colombes, not far from Nanterre, where we sometimes did our homework together. I loved it there when her Mum kindly served us tea and biscuits and treated us as adults. It was such a welcoming, warm feeling and I loved being in their nice, clean home. It was so much quieter than my home because here the family was so much smaller than my own. I really loved the friends I made during my time at Le Lycee. We were all working hard, trying to better our future by going to further education and it was nice to get the support of like-minded people.

During that time, I got really close to two of my teachers. One of them was my English teacher Mme Vecchini and my philosophy teacher who adored me as I was his favourite pupil and was often getting high marks from him. I really did love philosophy and sometimes when I re-read my own dissertations on a particular subject, I have difficulty recognising that it was me who actually wrote this amazing essay. Very often, I did not recognize either the style or the ideas I put down in writing. That always seemed to fascinate me as I was wondering where my inspiration came from to write so much about a philosophical subject.

Mme Vecchini helped me financially with the purchase of my books as at this point, my situation at home was rather delicate. If my parents found out what my studies cost them, they would immediately stop me without a moment's hesitation; they didn't need the extra expense and I wasn't a boy. So I hid the expenses from them and started to earn money babysitting in secret in my free school time so I could cover part of the costs. One day for my birthday, this wonderful Mme Vecchini offered me my first contact lenses as I still needed my glasses to see well and I was at an age where I paid much more attention to my looks, my body shape and the way I dressed, just like all my adolescents friends. I was always intrigued by the effect I had on men even then and as I was gradually becoming more and more attractive, it seemed men quickly "fell in love" with me and I very much enjoyed the attention I was getting from them.

I was very fond of Mme Vecchini and I loved the subject she was teaching us. For me, she was like a second mother, she wanted to help me succeed and she did a very good job at it. I was also her best pupil in class.

One day, I invited her to come to our home and eat the delicious dish of couscous my Mum kindly agreed to prepare for her. I wanted her to meet my family and perhaps she could pass the message on to my parents that I was a good student and they should let me carry on with my studies. My parents of course never understood her message or didn't want to. She loved my family and enjoyed the couscous immensely. This was the one and only time she ever came to my home.

I often visited her at weekends for lunch at her home at Portes d'Orleans in the south of Paris where she was living for years. I always enjoyed spending time with her talking about life, career and travelling. She was a breath of fresh air, bringing my dreams a little closer to reality. She followed me for quite some years later on in my life and was very proud of my progress. I am still in touch with her today.

During my time at Le Lycee, I also wanted to do more to help my brother Nasser who has Downs Syndrome. For my parents, he was like a permanent baby in an adult body, full of love and affection. Nasser could be stubborn though, an apparent family trait in most of us, he wasn't an exception and why should he be?

I liked that he was able to defend himself especially when my brothers teased him. He spent his days doing a paid manual job in a C.A.T (Centre d'Activite de Travail) located in Rueil Malmaison, the next commune to Nanterre, filling envelopes for mail slots.

Every day, he was picked up by shuttle in front of our high-rise and it was my Mum who took him downstairs, as he couldn't manage taking the lift by himself or be outside our home on his own. They collected him at 8:30 A.M. and dropped him back at 5 P.M. when someone from our home would be waiting for him to take him up in the lift. We lived on the third floor.

The C.A.T is Nasser's life and second home. There, he has many friends, and a few female admirers. I cared for my brother so much and very often at night time, I found myself in tears thinking about what kind of a life he was given – no life, no independence, no holidays, no activities. Is this his life? And why him? One day, I decided to do something for him and enrolled him in a special centre for disabled adults in Nanterre where I took him on Saturdays, a short bus ride away.

They had an activity for the day, either outdoors or indoors but more importantly; it was a day out for him doing something totally different instead of sitting around at home doing nothing constructive. I made sure he joined the same group for summer holidays and one year, decided to enrol myself as one of the helpers without asking my parents. My Dad didn't really like this of course and was ever so suspicious of the reasons why I wanted to do this. He thought I was only doing it as a means to get out of our home on Saturdays when normally I would be doing house chores.

After quite a bit of convincing, they eventually let me enrol him on a holiday to the seaside and I was going along as a helper with two other friends from my class at Le Lycee who happened to be free for the summer and wanted to help as volunteers.

The holiday came quickly. I was going with Nasser and my two girlfriends, I was very happy. It was the first time my parents let me go away by myself since my summer holidays in Belgium. It was my first time in such an environment too and the life amongst the disabled and the helpers was one I needed to get used to quickly and be totally part of. There was a lot of work in the kitchen, cooking, cleaning and making sure the participants were all well fed, clean, had taken their medication and were happy. At night once we had put them in bed, we all gathered together in one of the large rooms we had in the place we stayed at and someone played guitar and we all sang along. It was beautiful.

Team life was a big learning curve for me even though I came from a large family and at times, I found it a bit stressful as one needed quickly to adapt to different situations and resolve them then and there. I got close to one of the male helpers and it was a lovely experience until the day a new lady helper came and very quickly, he switched and *they* started a relationship. He was French and there was still a stigma attached to being associated with French born Algerians in France because of the past history of colonisation and lingering racism. It was very hurtful and disappointing because I did like him and he let me down.

My girlfriends who joined me on this trip also seemed to have got close to a couple of helpers but none developed into a serious relationship. In hindsight, it seemed we all needed a fair amount of emotional and moral support in this rather challenging environment and hang on to anyone who seemed normal to us.

Helping a group of disabled adults was very rewarding indeed but not easy at all both emotionally and physically. I was really happy to see my brother enjoy his time and he fitted into the group very well. It was also the first time he saw the sea and he was so frightened of the waves but slowly he got used to them.

With events unfolding soon after in my life, I never repeated this experience with him and no one in the family took over from me. I was really sad about this and for so many nights, I cried in silence just thinking about him and his quality of life. I couldn't understand how life could be so unfair.

At this stage, I seriously started to think about my life too and more specifically how I was going to live it. My inspiration came from famous actresses' lives like Audrey Hepburn and Marylyn Monroe to name but a couple. I so wanted to be a dancer, an airhostess or a midwife. The latter, my Mum was totally in favour of because she could relate to it having given birth so many times herself.

I spent three years at Le Lycee preparing for my A levels which was my biggest challenge but I was so determined to succeed and many nights, I studied until early morning. I was both excited and nervous at the same time because I was the only one in my family to go that far in school.

My Dad's frustration grew, the more I studied but that didn't matter so much anymore. I was determined to go on my life journey with or without him.

I was already feeling sad because the gap separating us was only about to get bigger. I had to hold on so tight as he pushed on with his insults and in my head, I started to question myself; should I continue or should I just give up? What was the point? Soon, I made a big decision and was going to show him what

I was capable of by completing my studies successfully and getting a good job. By now, he had lost hope with his boys; none followed further schooling and as for the girls, it didn't matter to him, he wasn't at all interested.

My three eldest sisters had been ordered to stop school when they reached an age when my Mum could use them to help with cooking, washing, and raising the young ones. Somehow, I passed through the system and fought for my right to study. It wasn't a favourable environment to prepare for an important exam like my A levels but I accepted my fate and dealt with it as best I could. I forged forward on my own and even my younger sister Alima wasn't inclined to follow in my footsteps. I already reeked of trouble.

For my Dad, I was a special case and he couldn't really understand what was motivating me. In his mind, my future, as for my other sisters, was already decided, I was going to get married and have kids and that was it.

My three years at the Lycee were quite tough for me, I was studying hard and sneaking into Paris in secret, I was falling in love with men who couldn't reciprocate my feelings and it was painful. My partner in crime was my best friend Zara. It was great to have her support and we had such good times together, sometimes laughing, very often crying.

The final year before A levels arrived, I was studying like crazy. I was very aware that I was good at some subjects but not so good at others. I studied long into the night preparing for exams until the last day and still I didn't feel I was completely ready. I was so nervous but I also realised that once the Baccalaureat was passed, a whole new world would open up for me with so many options for further studies, if only my parents let me. I went ahead with the preparation, sat the exams for various subjects over a week and finally, it was over and done.

One of my good friends, Naima was very keen to pass of course, like everyone else. She was a smart student and I had a lot of respect for her, she came from a much more liberal family than mine and had a lot of encouragement from her family for her exams, unlike me. We were anxiously waiting for our results for which we had to wait a whole month. Then the day of our results finally arrived.

We rushed to the notice board where our names were listed and the results shown right next to it. I found my name and I was sliding my shaking finger across to the results when I read *passé* (passed). I was immediately overwhelmed with joy - I had done it, I succeeded! I couldn't believe it. I can't explain the wonderful feeling that passed through my body, it was amazing.

At the same time, Naima found her name and against her name, it read *echoué* (failed). I was so disappointed that she didn't pass as we prepared almost all our subjects together. I could see how totally distraught she was! I didn't know what to do or say to her. Just that she needed to sit the exams again in two months' time and I promised I was going to help her.

I got home that day and told my Mum who was genuinely happy for me but my Dad didn't show any particular emotion. To my surprise, my Mum presented me with the most beautiful gift and voiced a *youyou*, a sound made by the rapid movement of the tongue inside the mouth used in Muslim celebration. I was thrilled, she was happy for me. I was in possession of the only gift she gave me in her lifetime and mine. It was a golden necklace with a butterfly pendant. It was beautiful *and it was a gift from Mum*. Sadly, many years later, I lost it in burglary at my flat in London.

It was during this time that my Uncle Amar went on his pilgrimage to Mecca, preparing for a return to his home in Algeria, and retiring from his work in France. He was going to look after his family there having been away from them for over fifteen years. I was saddened to lose such a wonderful uncle but I was also so very happy for him for he achieved his mission of saving enough money to complete building his home there and marrying off his children. I found out later, one of his secret desires was to have me married to one of his good sons whom I liked a lot but I couldn't see myself living in the Sahara desert leading a totally different life from the one I had in France.

When he came back from Mecca, he brought me a beautiful silver Allah pendant, which I cherished so much until it was also lost in the same burglary in London. Losing those sentimental pieces was awful, they had great emotional significance for me and for a while, I felt anger towards the burglars. But it soon passed and one suddenly realises that in fact one can live a happy simple life without the possessions one accumulates over the years and gets attached to.

Chapter 4

You will free yourself when you learn to be neutral and follow the instructions of your heart without letting things perturb you.

THE ESCAPE

I could clearly see that studying was a way of changing my future for the better. I even tried to convince my younger brothers of this, and more precisely, Hassan, Kamal and Mohamed. My message didn't seem to reach them at all and one day as I continued attempting to convince them, they threatened to hit me if I persisted.

I was shocked because they were, at least once, my smaller brothers now much taller and bigger than me. At that point, I sat down and thought to myself that this was it! I was done with my mission of trying to save them especially if they couldn't see it. I couldn't help them anymore and I began to think just for myself from then on.

Soon after that realisation, there came a point where I decided right or wrong, that I had to make a choice between the life my parents had in store for me or the life I wanted for myself. It was a very difficult choice but I knew deep inside that it was one I had to make.

I decided that my life was significantly more important since my parents were already more than half way done with their lives. After quite a lot of convincing, my parents finally allowed me to go to Nanterre University (Paris X), the nearest one to our home.

I was so thrilled as I was the only one of nine children who would go there and more importantly I was a girl. Whilst I was studying there for an English BA, I started to imagine a route of escape where I could start a new life somewhere in France, continue my studies, and live the way I wanted.

My current life, I thought, was too oppressive for me. I could never go out at night and I could never go out during the day without lying to my parents that it was a school trip and I was getting tired of lying. Why should I have to lie when all I was doing was bettering my future, there were so many things I wanted to do.

Over many sleepless nights, I formulated a plan of escape in my head and got a friend and a neighbour involved to help me get my clothes and books out of my parents' home discreetly.

At the time, I thought this was my only choice, my parents never accepted letting me go to live away from them if I wasn't married. My only option was to run away without anyone in my family noticing. In fact, jokingly, I asked my sister Farida if she would join me and we could start a new life somewhere else; she categorically refused of course, thinking I was mad. By her response, I knew I had to do this alone since my younger sister Alima was too young even though she was very smart and could see what was happening. If they caught me with her running away, I could get into trouble for corruption of a minor. I was scared and extremely anxious but determined to do it. Maybe it *was* madness, but it was so clear in my head that this was the way to go.

By now, my Dad had a hemi-paralysis after medical mistakes I believe took place whilst he was having a hospital check-up on a lump on his neck once he had retired from his very hard physical work.

Unfortunately, he was left unable to use his right side and completely dependent on my Mum who looked after him with so much love and care, washing and feeding him with all our help as well because it was so much hard work. My mother was also getting on and she wasn't the strong woman she once was now she was looking after my Dad and Nasser. We never understood what happened at the hospital but it left us with such a bitter taste for the French hospital care system.

I continued with my plan and my dream, which was to wait until my Mum went on holidays to Algeria in August 1983. I had just completed two years at University studying English Literature with one more year to go to acquire my BA. With my now frail Dad at home and no one paying attention, I managed to get my most important books and clothes out of our flat.

At first, I put them at my neighbour's home on the first floor she was a trustworthy lady who was about to play a big part in my escape. She was aware of the risk and still she was willing to help me. She was a very powerful woman both in stature and in character with a great sense of justice ingrained in her.

My belongings were now safely at her place waiting for a friend of mine to come and take them to his place. I was going to live with him until I got myself sorted with a secure home somewhere safe.

He was the first person with whom I started to discuss my plan and immediately he empathised with my situation even though we were not going out together. We agreed a day and a location when he was going to come and get me. All was looking really good and going according to plan. I was both very excited and very nervous about what I was about to do but kept on with my plan. After all, I was on my own in this with no support from my siblings whatsoever, not knowing where I was going from here.

Only one thing was crystal clear at the time; I wanted out of this family looking for a new and better life not knowing how and where, completely trusting the Universe. I was going with my intuition and the dream I had of the life I could have away from here.

In the meantime, my Mum returned from her holidays to Algeria refreshed and relaxed, happy to see us. I felt more sad for her than my Dad, as what I was about to do was anathema and scandalous in this tight community, putting my life at risk if it went wrong!

The day of the escape came and to my surprise, as I was getting ready to get out of our flat to go to my course which was my excuse to go out, my Mum stopped me saying my Dad said I couldn't go out! She instructed me to return to my room. At first, I was shocked and was wondering what was going on and if by chance, they had worked out my intent.

Unbeknownst to me, my Mum was looking for something

in the wardrobe where I normally keep my clothes and books and noticed that most of my things had gone! She immediately suspected that I was going to run away. From that day onward, my life turned into a nightmare.

They locked me in the bedroom and they also locked the front door so I couldn't get out. Until that point, I was still wondering what was going on, I felt cocooned in a strange sense of peace and calm even though I knew by now that my plan had failed and the consequences could be very serious and it quite possibly could be the end of my life as I knew it. It was, in other words, the beginning of a slow death.

I heard murmuring on the other side of the door and my Mum, without even trying to reason with me like she normally did, decided to share the double bed with me, just in case I was going to jump three floors down onto the front garden of our building to escape. Actually, this thought did cross my mind as the events unfolded. At this point, I felt I had nothing to lose, I didn't know what they would do to me, or where I was going to end up. I felt it was the end of my life.

The confinement around me increased, my Mum with me in the room and my sister Farida just outside the room sitting on the floor. I was totally trapped with no apparent way to escape. They started to search my bags for clues as to what I was up to. Really, they wanted to know if there was a man behind my reason to leave. Many girls made such crazy escapes for love, so when they found contraceptive pills in my bag, their fears were confirmed even though I had never taken any or slept with a man. All I wanted was to go away and continue my studies so I could better my future.

By now, they had taken all the contents of my bag away so I lost my address book with all the phone numbers of my close friends and my journal. I was never to see these again and losing all contact with my friends was really hard.

The next day, my brother Fawzy and my sister Farida drove me to the Algerian embassy to make a new passport as I refused to produce mine and it was nowhere to be found. They held both my hands from behind whilst walking outside and I felt like a real prisoner. The truth was that I had hidden my passport and there was no way I was going to hand it over to them, it was my escape route out of the country and into the world.

At home, we were not supposed to keep our own passports. They were kept in a safe with other family documents in my Mum's closet. I searched for it a few days earlier, found it and kept it hidden under the mattress in my room.

I knew they would come for it so I wrapped it in a plastic bag and threw it out of the window very close to the wall to avoid discovery. I then engaged my youngest brother Yasin to go and find a white plastic bag which he had to give to my neighbour downstairs who knew what was happening. My brother didn't know what was in the bag. I had passed a message on a piece of paper to my neighbour via my youngest sister Alima who wanted to help me, unlike Farida who was totally panicking; her future could also be affected because of my failed attempt to run away.

If my plan of escape failed, all the girls might be sent to Algeria as a consequence. That day, we came out of the Algerian Consulate with my new passport and yes, they were planning to take me to Algeria and leave me there to get married and raise children whilst caring for a husband.

I already decided suicide was my only solution if I was ever to end up there. Later on, I discovered that a French male friend of mine, who had seen potential of a supermodel in me, came looking for me. He was worried he hadn't heard from me. I am not sure how he found out where I lived but "where there is a will there is a way".

Unbeknownst to him I was in trouble; my brothers chased him away, stealing his wallet in case there was any useful information there about my plans. The poor man was in total panic and ran away as fast he could.

At that point, my situation was getting worse, with me in prison in my parents' home and with no outside help whatsoever. They were going to do with me what they wanted.

Then, one night, my Mum came to my room and asked me to spread my legs open. At first, I was a little surprised at this request. Of course, it was my father who had sent her to check if I was still a virgin. At that point, I hadn't slept with any men so she was happy with the result and went back to report to him.

For some mysterious reason up to now, I was surrounded by a complete sense of calm even though my situation didn't look good at all, in fact quite the opposite. I felt as if something much bigger than myself was protecting me and instinctively knew I was going to be fine, somehow.

At that point, I was left with no choice but to find a way to call the police for help. It was an extremely hard decision to make as this was my family but it was either that or I was finished forever.

I later learned the friend who was supposed to pick me up and take me away had come around my high rise on the day and at the precise time we agreed but after waiting for hours, he went away.

Luckily, he had met my neighbour downstairs who was keeping my stuff that he was supposed to load into his car. She told him about my situation from the note I had managed to pass down to her with my passport. I sent another note with my younger sister to her asking them to call the police for help. What followed was a waking nightmare never to be lived again.

The next day, everything was quiet in the flat with my departure for Algeria imminent – my brother Fawzy was so proud of himself taking charge of the situation instead of my father, feeling like a man. He nearly strangled me when I refused to tell him where I had hidden my passport and had bruises all over my neck as a consequence.

Unexpectedly, when the day approached for my departure and the flight was booked, my mother turned around and said to my Dad, in a very assertive tone, 'If she goes, I go too'. When I heard that, I was utterly shocked; my Mum never ever stood up to my Dad this way before. Deep inside, I was so very proud of her!

The next day was another quiet day as arrangements for my future were being made, when suddenly in the afternoon came a loud knock at our front door. I immediately knew what was happening and started to panic – how was I ever going to forgive myself?

They opened the door and two armed policemen dressed in plain clothes walked into our flat asking for me by name. I was locked in the back bedroom and started to shake.

One of them made his way to my room and wanted to speak to me, closing the door behind him whilst the other one made sure everyone kept calm reassuring them that all they wanted to do was speak with me. They *were* armed and that scared everyone in the house.

Of course, the question the policeman asked me immediately was, "Do you want to go or do you want to stay?" I looked at him with a white face and kept repeating they would kill me even being escorted by them between the room and the front door. How were they going to do that? I knew I wanted out, but not in this dramatic way. It was too late now; the situation was really bad and dangerous, since the policemen would not hesitate to use their weapons if violence broke out.

I had to think quickly but knew very well that I had reached the point of no return; they were here now, and for my safety I had to go *with* them. Seeing how terrified I was he tried to calm me down and reason with me. After a few minutes, we were ready to go.

He held me firmly by my arm, walked me out of our flat, full of family memories and which I never was going to come back to!

I really felt sorry for my parents at this point, especially my poor mother who was screaming so loud for me not to go, she was joined by two of my older sisters shouting at me that I was completely mad and where did I think I was going.

The policemen tried to calm them down saying they were going to take me to their office for a talk and to reassure them, asked if someone could come with me. My sister Farida volunteered. My brothers were away at the moment, which was a very good thing, as the situation could have escalated dangerously with them around.

We left, and as soon as we drove off, I felt an overwhelming sense of freedom. I knew I was never going back. I had escaped and the only clothes I had with me were the shabby Arabic dress I wore at home for the last few days and a headscarf. I had no money, no papers – where was I going to go? What was I going to do?

Of course, as soon as we reached *la Prefecture de Police de Nanterre* (Police Headquarters), they asked my sister to leave. She was absolutely furious and started to insult them. They calmly walked her out, their mission was to get me out safely and they had succeeded.

We were sure my brothers would come looking for me there that night so for my protection, they locked me in a cell overnight just in case they attempted to harm me. I discovered later, they did come but didn't get to me. There was an exchange of insults between them and the policemen but they eventually left. By that time, I was so exhausted I just drifted off into a deep sleep until the next morning.

The police officers located my friend Dieudonne who was supposed to come to get me. I was amazed at how a friend can risk his life entering into a crazy plan such as this, unaware of the possible consequences. He turned up the next day and drove me safely to freedom, far away from Nanterre.

I opened the car window and felt the fresh air, feeling so relieved, happy and thanking the Universe and everyone who had come to my rescue. This was the beginning of a new life and I didn't know what was in store for me, but I had faith that all would be well.

I stayed in contact with one of the police officers that came to my rescue; he wanted to know how I was getting on. My friend offered me a bed whilst I was sorting myself out and planning to continue my studies. Obviously, I couldn't go to my local University in Nanterre Paris X any longer as it was very close to where my family lived. I knew my brothers would continuously search for me there and everywhere else they could think of. Later, I heard they looked for me for two years before giving up.

I ended up registering at the University of Paris Saint Denis, far enough away that no one could trace me. Whilst Nanterre was to the west of Paris past the financial district of La Defense, Saint Denis was in the north of Paris. I had to be on the train for an hour and a half coming from Evry, in the southeast of Paris. I felt safe there and was confident no one could find me. I settled into a little routine going to my classes at the University, switching from train to metro in the centre of Paris at Gare de Lyon.

My heartbeat always sped up in panic when I reached this station in the centre of Paris there was a good chance that I might bump into someone from my former life there. I passed through quickly, keeping my head down. One day though, as I made my way to the metro from the train station, I suddenly felt a tap on my shoulder and my world came to a halt. I turned my head and it was my friend Dieudonne. I think he didn't realize how much he scared me and I yelled at him never to do it again, at least not in Paris.

As my confidence grew, I considered moving to another country. Dieudonne's brother-in-law, a radio broadcaster, was willing to help with some contacts he had at the Town Hall to expedite getting a French passport. With that, I could leave freely and live and work in any other country in the European Community I chose. I held an Algerian passport at that time, the one which survived my family search. We began the application procedure and even then it took nearly a year before I could get my French passport, the system was that slow.

I prayed nothing bad would happen to me whilst waiting for my new passport, and my family would not find me. If they did, I believed it could truly be the end of my life this time. I also was very aware at this precise moment, my family, especially my parents, were suffering not knowing where I was or indeed if I was still alive and that saddened me.

After a few months into my new life, my friend introduced me to The Rosicrucian Fellowship, an esoteric organisation helping in the development of psychic powers as he knew I had an interest there. I went to an introductory meeting and liked the people. I joined them and started to study the various booklets they sent us weekly. We paid a small monthly membership to receive the information and to be able to attend the meetings. I found this circle of people so interesting and enjoyed their company since it was also a support network for me. At last, I was free to do those things I was interested in without anyone trying to stop me.

Whilst I was studying at the University of Saint Denis, I had the opportunity to meet and become friends with Suha Tawil who later became Yasser Arafat's wife and gave him a son. She introduced me to her Palestinian family who were very kind and extremely interesting people to me, especially her mother, an eminent journalist and writer fighting for her country and exiled to France to protect herself and her family. I really felt privileged to have been able to share some time with them and discuss many a political subject.

Sadly, once Suha got married to Yasser Arafat, I lost touch with her. They moved to Tunisia where the security blockade around her was very tight. I was both disappointed and sad I could not get in touch with her again and still am to this day.

During the time that I was waiting for my passport to be ready, I discovered the pleasures of sex. This forbidden act I was not allowed to explore whilst with my family. Dieudonne and I got close and started a relationship, which was never going to last forever, because we were quite different.

One day though, I discovered I was pregnant. I was twenty-two years old and my life had just started, there was no way I was going to become a mother just now.

I got into a real panic; it was so stupid of me to have got into such a situation after all I had been through. It was too late to reason, it was action time, so I decided to have an abortion without consulting him. He was furious when I returned from the hospital. In his mind I had just killed his child. After that, our relationship went sour. In his rage, he managed to steal money from my bank account by forging my signature. I totally trusted this man who played such a crucial part in my rescue. I couldn't believe it.

Shortly after this, my French passport came through. I decided to take off and move to London for a while, just the time I needed to get myself back together after this episode. By then, I almost had completed my BA in English Literature and my great teachers agreed I could finish it by distant learning with them. I was so grateful to them as this was something they didn't normally do for their students, who usually had to be present in classes to complete a degree.

A few months before I moved to London, my grant stopped and I had to find a way to earn a living. My good friend Suha introduced me to the owners of a small Lebanese shop in Paris, near Le Jardin du Luxembourg, where I ended up working part-time. They sold the most delicious Middle Eastern delicacies. I was happy there and learned how to use the till and serve clients. Kamal, the brother of the lady owner also worked there summers while he was studying in Germany and we ended up becoming lovers.

I loved the idea of coming to an area of Paris where I thought no one could find me. It gave me a true sense of freedom, but it had come at such a price; I had lost contact with my dear friends from Nanterre after my address book was taken away from me – but I simply HAD to keep moving for my own safety and survival.

Chapter 5

A man can't be the judge of his neighbour's intelligence.
His own vital experience is never his neighbour's.

LONDON

London... the city which saved and made me

I was 24 years of age when I packed all my things into a suitcase and took the overnight bus, crossing the Channel by ferry to reach central London the next day. I didn't tell Dieudonne where I was heading. I arrived at Victoria Station, ending up in Earls Court which is where I started my London life. At first and for quite a while, I felt totally lost with no family or friends around. What was I going to do now? Where should I start? I had nowhere to live and had no work.

It took me quite a few months to adjust. I first stayed in a youth hostel just off Earls Court Road where there was plenty of life in the streets and I slept in a dormitory with eight other girls.

I felt vulnerable and exhausted, having fought so hard against such a large family. I now had the whole world in front of me but I really didn't know what to do with it. My English was pretty good so I could easily communicate with people and was able to investigate the possibilities of getting a job, so that I could pay for my lodging.

I approached most of the hotels in Earls Court for any work they might have. Finally, I ended up working at a hotel just off Earls Court Road where I became good friends with the receptionist, Eric from Ghana. He was working there evenings to earn money so he could finish his Master's Degree. We became really close friends and Eric gave me a lot of support during those early, hard times in London. I had uprooted myself to a country with a different language and a totally different culture - I still wasn't sure how long I was going to stay there.

We took a few trips around England and spent many a New Year's Eve dancing the night away in some of the nice clubs in Kensington High Street. He was such a gentle and kind man and I enjoyed his friendship immensely. I also had the chance to meet his young boss, Mohamed who was from India. These two became my good friends and it was nice to have them nearby to give me the feeling that I belonged somewhere again.

For two years, I lived in a tiny room in a house in Warwick Road owned by a Indian man. To make his home more profitable, he divided all the rooms in half. The separating wall was so thin I could hear everything going on in the next room. I discovered my next door neighbour was from Portugal and was working very long hours to send money back to his family to pay for the home he was building there.

Often, I heard him when he got into bed as he either snored or cleared his throat, making horrible, disgusting sounds. We didn't have a kitchen and we shared toilets and a bathroom with others (mostly men) living there. I never knew how many we were in total. I found a little stove for my room so I could at least make tea or coffee, boil an egg or heat up soup. I was already saving money to be able to move to a better place but I liked Earls Court, a place full of life and many things to do.

I came and went freely and fairly safely. There were groups of Australians that seemed to spend their life drinking themselves silly in the local pubs. I had never seen people get so drunk before and it was something of a shock to me.

I decided to buy a typewriter to teach myself how to type. It seemed that the only way I could qualify for an office job was to be able to type. By that time, I had completed my BA in English Literature and I was really so proud of myself. I had achieved my mission.

I constantly tried to find ways to better myself and decided to take a computer course in Holborn, central London in the hope this qualification might help me get the office job I wanted. There, I met the lovely Souad Babaamer who I found to my delight had come by herself to London from Algeria, to learn

English and computer skills. I admired her parents for allowing her to travel alone to a foreign country. I often reminded her how lucky she was to have such trusting parents unlike my own backward thinking ones in France.

Why were they that way? Perhaps they were trying to hold onto a cultural identity they left behind when they immigrated to France. But they failed to realise that, their culture continued to evolve whilst they stagnated.

We quickly became very good friends and spent a lot of time together until the day she finally had to return home to Algiers. I found her to be quite open minded and smart compared to the Algerian girls I grew up with in France.

Amusingly, those girls had a tendency to make up stories about their success at school and later on at work, just to impress. It upset me when I realised what they were doing. Why did they have to boast about something they didn't even have or own? I was doing the complete opposite, playing down my achievements to avoid feelings of jealousy or envy in them. Staying modest at all times was my motto, it helped to avoid unnecessary attention.

So life in London was slowly shaping up. I started a little routine, going to a fitness club for aerobics classes, making new friends and thinking of how to improve my job situation all the time. I finally landed my first office job with a public relations company, Blackburn Willett and Associates, run by a lovely lady of my age whom I admired so much. I was so impressed with her and often wondered how such a young and beautiful woman could become successful and run her own business.

When she offered me the job, I accepted her invitation to go for a drink at her home where she offered me a glass of champagne. She and her husband owned a beautiful home in Fulham, in the South West of London. She had everything I ever wished for and I had tremendous respect for her. I enjoyed working in her office overlooking the River Thames in Hammersmith. It was a small office with only two other ladies working there. I walked to work stopping for a swim at my gym on the way, feeling nicely refreshed for a day at work.

I was hoping to be able to use my French in the job as she had a couple of French clients but the European Community was just opening up and they were only looking to promote their products within the UK.

I remember upsetting one of my colleagues once by correcting her English grammar but the mistakes were so obvious to me and I couldn't help pointing them out to her. After all, how could a foreigner be better at English than a native? The truth was that I had learned English grammar in depth and perhaps they hadn't.

I worked in this office for a year before I moved on to my next PR job with Communique on the Kings Road, in central London. Now that I had a regular income, I decided to move to a bigger place sharing a big house with seven other women in Willesden Green, North London. I had a large room there, with a double bed, a wardrobe and a desk where I could study since I decided to take on a diploma course in Business Communication, attending evening classes.

I lived on the first floor with four other girls sharing one bathroom and toilet. I really enjoyed their company but found it difficult to accept that cleaning standards varied so much from one person to the other! Even though we set a weekly cleaning schedule, some of my housemates didn't bother with their turn which irritated me. Apart from that, life in Willesden Green was very enjoyable and I was now commuting by underground to get to my job in Chelsea - a daily commute of a little over an hour each way.

Working on the Kings Road opened my eyes to the consumer world. Seeing all those beautiful people dressed in the latest fashion walking up and down this popular street full of designer shops fascinated me. Very often, celebrities were spotted on the street but I only recognised them when someone pointed them out to me.

I loved Kings Road and started to imagine that one day I too, would live in this neighbourhood. My job at Communique was good and I really started to use my skills in a satisfying way. I was exposed to office politics for the first time and at first, I didn't understand the need for these dynamics. Later on, I realised it happened in most office environments. I was gradually given more and more responsibilities and my social life was getting more and more exciting, going out and making new friends. Many I met at the various evening courses I joined to increase my chances of progressing to manager level. At least, at that time, I thought that should fulfil my life ambition and make me really happy. Was I wrong?

One day, my good friend Eric came to meet me for lunch on the Kings Road and I could see he wasn't his normal self. When pressed, he confessed he had visa trouble, which could mean that he might be expelled from the country any time soon. One way to resolve this problem was for him to marry a European person. So, without hesitation and in pure desperation, he asked me if I would agree to a marriage of convenience with him. I paused, shocked at first because I never thought of him as husband material and I wasn't sure that once married, he would go ahead with a divorce as agreed because I knew he liked me a lot.

It was hard as I could see he was stuck but I couldn't go through with it. It simply wasn't part of my plan. I felt badly for a few days, putting myself in his shoes. What could I do? My wish was to marry only once in my life and in my head, I figured, if I married late, I had less chance of experiencing divorce! Eric was so deeply hurt by my refusal but he knew not to force me with such issues.

A year had passed in London. I often missed my family but believed for my own protection, I shouldn't get in touch with them, I couldn't be sure of their reaction. I stayed away from them for a total of seven years. However, during that time, I became very close to one of my French sisters-in-law, Martine, whom my parents already accused of influencing my decision to leave.

I called her regularly to hear news from my parents and family. She was extremely discreet and I trusted her totally. I was so glad to be able to speak to her, she was the only family

I could talk to. I was happy when she told me my parents were okay and still alive. My biggest fear was not seeing them again before they passed away. I wanted to make peace with them some day soon.

I also discovered my brother Hassan was going through a life crisis, becoming homeless, drinking and taking tranquilisers the doctor prescribed for him. He was one year my junior and was one of the most resourceful brothers I had. He enjoyed managing the various grocery shops he worked in and I could imagine him running his own shop one day.

Because of the trauma of the separation from my family, I suffered some physical discomfort for quite a few years which manifested as a thick, small ball lodged in my throat as if holding back feelings that needed to be expressed. To help, I joined a course of self-development which claimed to release stored anger and resentment. I found a place at the Power House in Chelsea close to my work and enrolled in their weekend course. It was there for the first time, I came to terms with parts of myself I didn't know existed, letting go of deep issues that weren't working for me any longer. It seemed I had so much repressed anger, which once released through various exercises during the course, allowed me to feel more at peace.

Many of my objectives were achieved on this course and it was also where I met John with whom I was to spend the next ten years of my life. John was a very special and unusual character, often thinking outside the box, very intuitive and not afraid of saying what he thought. I was fascinated by his self-confidence. He was also blessed with very beautiful blue eyes and soon we were dating.

I worked with him in his office in Clapham's Falcon Road whilst hunting for my next job opportunity. John supported me, along with a couple of other dear friends from the group, in resolving many personal issues.

In 1990, I finally secured a job, which was to be the beginning of my international career. It seemed all my previous jobs were preparing me for this move. The job location was in Fulham, just off Munster Road in South West London, where I worked before. With John's persistence and great power of persuasion, I moved in with him in a nice and spacious flat off Northcote Road in Battersea, South West London. With him, I started my first live-in relationship with a man and it was a big deal especially coming from such an oppressed and male dominated background.

John was a gentle man who took pleasure in cooking and eating which explained his round body shape. Most mornings, he walked to the local market just off our street to buy fresh ingredients and prepare a most delicious breakfast for us. We were both cyclists and every day, I cycled forty five minutes to my office in Fulham, burning calories and shedding all the extra body fat I accumulated since my arrival to London. I really enjoyed finally having a place I could call 'home' and which I didn't have to share with so many other people. Following my dream, I started to buy decorative items for our flat, replacing existing ones that didn't suit our taste.

Leaving the house in Willesden Green was sad though but I knew it was the way to go on with my life, moving in the right direction. In fact, I later became really good friends with a couple of my ex-housemates especially, a delightful Turkish lady called Gehidi who occupied the room next door. She was older than me and was an example of the lady I wanted to become. She was a pharmacist, very tidy, beautiful, kind and very smart. We stayed friends for a long time until the day I completed my self-development course.

It seemed she couldn't cope with the obvious changes in me and she withdrew within for self-protection. I kept in touch with her later when she moved into a cute studio flat she bought in Willesden, achieving one of her own dreams. I visited her there a few times but eventually lost touch.

Life with John though was pleasant. We went for long walks in the two London parks we had in walking distance from our flat. There were large family houses in our area and I dreamed one day, one of these would be mine. We played tennis and talked a lot. John's thinking and reasoning was quite unusual and made discussions with him refreshing. He had a totally unique way of looking at situations and people. We also had a nice circle of friends whom we met with regularly for dinner and to share ideas.

Very often, we went to Glastonbury to visit John's mother. She was the most amazing new age woman I had ever met in my life, running a small guest house and offering treatments including massage, healing and rebirthing to name a few. She had married at least five times to attractive and much younger men who usually ended up working with her in the business. She also had a new age bookshop in the town centre, which was doing reasonably well.

I really enjoyed going there weekends taking the National Express bus from Victoria station and enjoying the ride out of London heading for the country, appreciating the beauty of the English scenery on the way.

Arriving in the countryside from London was such a blissful experience. We walked, ate, played, and relaxed, getting recharged for our return to bustling London town.

Because of where we met, John knew almost everything about my family story and he was the one who finally encouraged me to reconcile with them after all these years of separation. One day, I learned from Martine that my family gave up searching for me and all my parents wanted to know was if I was alive and well. Perhaps, they suspected we were in touch. I often daydreamed of returning to them as a very successful business woman, owning my own home and even buying a home for them as I knew this was one my Dad's most cherished dreams and wishes.

After one year living together in Battersea, John and I decided to purchase our first flat in Streatham, a little further south from where we were. An interior decorator occupied it so the flat was nicely done with really good taste. It was a two bedroom flat with a cellar and a small garden with a tree.

Although this was an important accomplishment for me, once I found myself in the flat with John, a great sense of claustrophobia overwhelmed me and I felt like running ... what had I done? Was I to be with this man for the rest of my life? The next few years were quite a challenge for us as a couple since I always found excuses not to go any deeper in our relationship. We managed to survive because we were good friends, supporting each other in times of need and I enjoyed his companionship a lot. With time though, we slowly grew apart as we had such different interests.

I was making progress in my career, started to travel with my job, started yoga, socialised and saw a lot of my friend Mariejoe from Chile who was working in London at the time. Meanwhile, he sat in front of the TV watching his favourite football team play on weekends. He probably was very content in our cosy environment but I needed more stimulation. I was naive to think a couple did almost everything together and realised we were very different we didn't have many things in common.

Chapter 6

REUNION

Around 1993, I was ready to reconcile with my family. I had my home, my man, my job and was successfully 'settled'. My plan was to first make a phone call to my mother and then take it from there. It took me quite a few weeks to prepare myself for this psychologically. The first time I spoke to my mother over the phone, I was sitting in a meeting room at work. We had just moved to new offices near Victoria Station. It was a quiet afternoon in the office and I went to an unoccupied meeting room from where I could make the call without being disturbed.

With shaky hands, I dialled my parents' home number which I knew by heart and Farida picked up the phone. I could hear from her voice she was in total shock, didn't know what to say and very quickly passed me on to my Mum. When my poor Mum heard my voice, she couldn't believe it, her voice was trembling and she burst into tears. I couldn't hold my tears back either and was thrilled to hear her voice, realising she was well but didn't know what else to tell her on the phone. I made a promise to come and visit her soon. It was a huge breakthrough for me and I was really happy to have done it as I was wondering if I ever would have the courage to call her. Thanks to Martine I did, and I will be grateful to her for a long time to come even though sadly she is not with us anymore.

Back in London, life was improving and I felt more like a normal human being and enjoyed life more fully, perhaps for the first time having reconnected with part of me. However, I was very ambitious on the career front and wanted to climb the corporate ladder as quickly as possible, feeling I was already quite behind some of my peers having been hindered by serious personal circumstances. It was through my Fulham PR work my career veered towards international export business.

By now, I qualified in Export Management through attending evening classes and was very proud of myself. After all, this was where I wanted to be so I could use all my language skills and travel extensively within Europe. The job opened up new avenues for me, expanding my horizons starting with using English and French on the phone. Even though I learned Spanish during my three years in High School, until now I hadn't the chance to use it, so this language decided to hibernate somewhere in a secret part of my brain until it was needed again. I decided to bring it back to life by going on an intensive two weeks language course in Valencia in Spain. I knew once I returned from this trip, I had to use my Spanish regularly.

An idea came to mind when I returned and I put up a notice at a language school five minutes away from my work, looking to exchange conversation with one of their language students. The idea was to spend two lunch hours weekly, one speaking only in English and the other one, Spanish. It was great fun and ended up becoming very best friends with Mariajose Balmaceda, a.k.a. Mariejoe from Santiago in Chile.

Meanwhile, plans for visiting my parents were being made and John bravely agreed to accompany me to my parents' home because I was quite nervous and didn't know what to expect. I also was a bit nervous we would find ourselves in a dangerous situation. However, it was such a big deal he came since not only was he English but also a man and a big one too!

I wanted them to see I was okay and settled in my life so they wouldn't worry about me. The date was agreed upon with Hanan, December 1990; she kindly proposed to come and pick us up from the nearest train station in Nanterre – Nanterre Université which I knew so very well from my university days there.

On the day, we got ready and left for this adventure together. I really admired John for coming along with me, and not being afraid of something going wrong, he was either so trusting or ignorant. However right now, he was my rock and I needed that. We travelled almost an entire day to get to Paris by boat and train and had arranged to stay at a friend's place in the expensive part of Paris from where we could enjoy the sights. It was John's first trip to France and we wanted to make the most of it.

The cold winter's morning broke and I was preparing myself psychologically to see my parents, what was I going to tell them? Would I still recognise them? We had a good breakfast in our cosy Parisian flat just off the glamorous Champs Elysées, then started our journey towards Nanterre where my family was expecting us for lunch.

As the RER train was nearing Nanterre Université, my heart started to race uncontrollably, I was nervous and a bit scared of what I was going to see and hear. We got off the train and everything appeared the same as I had left it years before. Nanterre Université brought back so many memories from my time there. As promised, Hanan was waiting for us in her car. We were only a short ride from my parents' flat. She seemed very happy to see me and I saw she hadn't changed much.

It was a strange feeling for me to step back into Nanterre after so long and flashbacks of my last few days there couldn't help but resurface. What if this was a big mistake again? What if we were never to come out of Nanterre alive? They could set a trap; so many frightening scenarios came to my mind. It was already very nice to see my sister who was so very thrilled.

We finally reached my parents' building when my stomach and throat tightened so much I couldn't speak anymore. Realizing this, John was very supportive and encouraging even though he couldn't totally understand everything about my past nor speak any French. No more boys gathered downstairs in the lobby like they used to do. Those I left were now hopefully grown-ups doing well for themselves. Also the lobby colour was now a striking bright orange, not the colour I remembered.

We waited for the lift and went up to the third floor, it seemed to take forever. We reached the door and Hanan rang the bell. She seemed very proud of herself bringing me back to our parents. The last time I was at this door, I was fleeing for my life, but here I was again. Was I crazy?

Hearing the doorbell, my Mum came to open the door. I

could see a flash of emotion pass through her whole body when she put her eyes on me. She held me in her arms so tightly and wept. It was such a strange feeling for me too to see her again, and it felt like I had never left. She was older and little weaker. She mumbled a few things I couldn't understand then took me to my Dad who was now even frailer, sitting on his sofa in the lounge as usual. When I got to him, he was speechless and tearful and simply hugged me. He was relieved to see me in one piece.

It was very odd for John to witness such an emotional scene but we spoke about this subject before and he was prepared. Once we got accustomed to each other again, my parents started to ask questions about me, my life, where was I living? What was my job? Did I earn a lot of money? Did I buy a home? They were quite pleased with the answers I gave them, especially my Dad who never expressed his approval openly of what I did being a man with such great pride.

My Mum, being her usual generous hostess, provided us with delicious food, fresh mint tea, peanuts, and cakes. John observed the scene quite amused, as one by one, my brothers and sisters came to see me to say hello. They were as curious about me as I was about them. So far, the only person still missing was Farida who, to my surprise, was at work! Some things indeed improved since I was last here. At that time, considering work outside the home was a no-go situation, yet it seemed it was quite acceptable now.

I was pleased to see this positive change and was happy chatting to my siblings with whom I was trying to reconnect. No one dared voice the subject of what happened seven years back. There was no need for that; not now and not later. It happened, was in the past and now, as a family, we needed to move on.

After being fed all afternoon with the delicious couscous only my Mum knew how to make and catching up with everyone, it was time to leave.

With difficulty, John and I had to extricate ourselves from the family to go back to our friend's flat in the centre of Paris. I couldn't quite come to terms with the fact that I was free to go back to my life and they were not going to stop me anymore. Times had changed and I felt liberated and happy to have reconciled with my parents.

We stayed in Paris a few days, visiting my parents in Nanterre a few more times. Farida's working hours were quite long, and we kept missing her, so we agreed to meet up with her at a train station. We met her at La Defense which is quite a big station. When she saw me, she hugged me, bursting into tears and weeping with joy. She seemed shorter than I remembered her but she was well and very happy to see me at last.

After a few days in Paris, we returned home to South London and it felt like a huge burden had been lifted from my shoulders. I was at peace and very grateful to John for his support. Now I could carry on and try to lead a normal life.

My work-life in Fulham was progressing step by step and I felt I was on my way to the international career I longed for. For lack of confidence and stifling beliefs, my career progress seemed slow but I had a strategy that would eventually take me where I wanted to be. After all, I was qualified and I could speak three languages, a skill which was not easy to find in London at the time.

When I returned, I started to work on that and John helped me but I felt he was holding me back. He thought the jump from where I was to where I wanted to be was too big. He was a little obstacle compared to those I had already overcome.

I kept on believing in myself and improving skills that I thought were an asset and sure enough, I got my first international sales position. It was a good time to move as the atmosphere in the office where I was working began to change for the worse when the wife of my boss decided she was going to be my boss too, even though they operated two different companies and he was the one employing me.

By that time, my social life with my friend Mariejoe was buzzing and as she also lived in the area where I worked, I got to know her much better, doing various activities together, and sharing life experiences. No doubt, we became very close friends and I often spent nights over at her place, sleeping on a mattress on her floor. It was great fun for a while.

I continued visiting my parents on my own on a regular basis and my Mum spoiled me with food as her only way of showing me love. I had such a different life from my siblings now: working, travelling and doing exciting things. Every time I tried to share my experience with them, they either seemed uninterested or simply couldn't understand what I was talking about.

Strangely, every time I came back from my parents' home, I felt completely drained of my energies. It was like my strength was totally taken away from me. I couldn't explain it. Perhaps I was forcing myself to fit into a place where I didn't belong? I decided to reduce the frequency of visits to them. At the same time, I also decided to stop telling them my stories of travels and instead turned my attention to them, asking questions about their lives, something at least they could relate to.

In the meantime, my Dad was getting tired of depending on my Mum and being stuck at home all day. One morning, as he was looking for food in the pantry, he accidentally slipped and fell, hurting the good side of his body. He ended up in hospital for treatment but since then seemed to have lost all confidence in walking, he was bedridden by choice. His immobility started to cause him pressure ulcers that wouldn't heal even with medical attention and he was in a lot of pain. He was hospitalised for eight months and injected with an increasing dose of morphine to relieve his pain.

It was extremely painful for us to see him suffer without being able to help. I took time off work in London to come to visit him in hospital in Nanterre but he was getting weaker and soon he wasn't even able to speak with us.

He was fed intravenously and his lips and mouth were very dry so, we passed a wet Q-tip over his lips so that the skin would not break down and to keep his mouth moist. He seemed to recognize us (or so I hoped) despite the increased dose of morphine he was injected with daily.

Every night, one of my brothers was allowed to sleep over in his hospital room to keep an eye on him. He eventually gave up the fight and passed away one night at the end of October 1997. Strangely enough it was the only night no member of the family stayed over. Was this pure coincidence or was it some indirect help from the medical staff? I still wonder until this day. I was thankful to be around at this time, my biggest concern having not to be able to see him before he passed away. My strong Dad was gone. The man who once was both the biggest comfort and obstacle in my life didn't exist anymore. How was this possible? I couldn't understand. Where did he go? Could he see us? What was he telling us? What was he doing?

Even though we were expecting this for a while, it was a very sad moment for us all especially for my Mum. Following the Muslim tradition, my Dad's body was to be expatriated by plane to his home village where he was buried near his parents, brother and other members of his family. In France, almost all Algerian families save up money to have the bodies of their deceased flown back home for burial, a very costly tradition.

My Dad's death was the first one in our immediate family and it was a shock for all of us to experience it so closely. When I reached my parents' flat travelling from London, my Dad had already passed away. My Mum asked me to go to the morgue to say goodbye to the man who once was my Dad. At first, I refused to go as I had never seen a dead body before. I didn't know what my reaction was going to be but with the support and insistence of family friends, I gave in and went. In the Muslim tradition, the body is prepared to enter Heaven, clean. A religious person from the mosque comes to wash the body reciting prayers throughout the ritual, then the body is embalmed, preparing it for judgement in the after-world where it was decided if this soul should go to Heaven or be burned in Hell.

The body is then wrapped in a white sheet and the head bandaged leaving the face exposed. The body is then placed in the wooden coffin purchased by the family. It is now ready to be wheeled to the room where family and close friends are waiting to say their last words and goodbyes to the deceased.

When I approached my Dad's body, I said goodbye and asked

for forgiveness then bent to kiss his forehead. As I drew near, I could feel the air changing, a chill hung around him and as I brought my lips close to kiss him, I was shocked by the hardness and cold that death brought upon him who was always so warm. I was still so naive about death. I moved away quickly and left the room in tears. This was not how I wanted to remember him.

There was then a short administrative ritual to seal the coffin and confirm this person deceased. A specially equipped van waited outside to transport the coffin to the airport. There, it was loaded onto the same passenger flight as the family members accompanying it, destined for Algiers where other family members were waiting at the airport.

It was a very strange feeling to see this now lifeless body locked into a box never to be seen again standing in the flesh. For me, it once again confirmed the fragility of life and that we must all leave by same route, without exception. With my Dad gone, I felt he had taken a part of my life with him. I remained confused for a long while as now I had no one to rebel against anymore or prove anything to. I was now free to live my life the way I saw fit and for me but it was something I was learning to do slowly, over years after his passing.

Now my mother was truly alone. Perhaps for the first time in her life, she had to make decisions, looking after her grown children especially my problematic brother Hassan. Instinctively and protectively, we all drew closer to her to help ease her pain and make her feel less lonely. Luckily, she had very supportive friends who regularly visited her in the afternoons when she was on her own whilst Farida was at work.

I visited my Mum more often but it was hard. I quickly became bored in Nanterre with nothing to do except sitting and eating all day. During this time though, I got closer to my sisters Farida and Alima and in time, we started to organise nights out having some fun in Paris, something I could never do during my time living with my parents and I was glad things were different now.

My Mum asked questions about our outings but she knew she couldn't stop us anymore. We had a good time together and it was nice to have these bonding experiences, getting to know them again. I was even able to forgive Farida for letting me down at a crucial time of my life because of her own fears.

Whenever we can today, we still try to have our nights out. Farida was living with my Mum, Nasser and Sabir who was thrown out by his long term partner Martine with whom he had three daughters. Farida didn't get on at all with him, for unknown reasons. He decided to take on the role of the father ordering her around and she despised him so much for this. Things were never to get any better between them and they often got into big arguments as she fiercely and rightly defended herself. Luckily, my Mum was there to bring a stop to their fights.

During one of my visits, Sabir started an argument with her. When I intervened taking her side, of course, he lashed out at me and I soon ignored him, not tolerating such a macho attitude.

My life in comparison was rather refreshing; most men around me, including John, were normal and pretty domesticated. They didn't expect a woman to care for their basic needs like cooking and laundry as he did. I had no time for such old-fashioned men and felt truly sorry for Farida who lived with this daily.

In hindsight, it was this very attitude that I rebelled against all those years ago. Farida was waking up to this now and it was her turn to fight. On the other hand, Alima's way out was to get married to someone she met by herself. She gave birth to a daughter and it seemed she wasn't happy in her relationship so she decided to divorce her husband two years after their marriage. This in itself was a huge scandal in the family but she fought on and of course, I admired her for doing that. She soon met another man with whom she fell in love and decided to marry him.

My brothers stopped talking to her for a while because divorce simply was not acceptable and she had the courage to go through with it even against my Mum's advice. She lived one hour away from my Mum's place, with her new husband and was raising the first child she had with him; two more followed later.

Soon, it transpired that my Mum was scared of being on her own, she didn't feel secure in her third floor flat. Farida felt guilty and arranged for Hanan and her daughter to come and sit with her some afternoons whilst she was at work. My Mum was accustomed to being surrounded by family and friends and it was the first time she found herself truly alone, her life-partner now gone and her grown-up children caring for their own families.

She started manipulating Farida to stay with her all day and soon, Farida seriously considered resigning from her work to be with her. Farida needed to think about her life too though. Over the years, many marriage proposals came her way and each time she refused, feeling she couldn't leave my Mum alone and none seemed to suit her anyway At the time, well into her forties, her chances of getting married were getting slimmer by the day. Fortunately, she seemed happy, with lots of friends around and having a good time whenever possible. Even now, she expresses a certain *joie de vivre* and often smiles though childless and still unmarried.

Back in London, my life was vibrant with good career progression, a nice circle of friends, travelling, taking yoga classes and finally being able to enjoy life. I was always thirsty for knowledge and very often found something new to do or learn. On the other hand, John was very content with his home life and his work and I started to get bored at home. I was now going out a lot more without him and slowly, we grew apart, eventually sleeping in different rooms. One day, under pressure from my best friends who could see I was wasting my precious time, I told John that we would be better off living apart.

The only possession we had together was our flat in South West London. I was in my mid-thirties now and in my heart, I was confident that I had plenty of time to meet the right man with whom to raise the family I so wanted. John didn't have any savings to buy me out or to buy himself another flat so we lived under the same roof, apart, but good friends for four years whilst he was saving money to buy his own place.

During this time, I had a three-year long relationship with a man who was living with another woman. He claimed not to be happy with her and believed he wanted out so I agreed to start what turned out to be a truly fulfilling relationship with him in every way. When we got together, we talked for hours about various subjects of interest, travel, work, current affairs. We went away some weekends and stayed in amazing places around England, and we also travelled abroad.

One day, I got pregnant by him accidentally and because he didn't want any family responsibilities he was not interested in having a child, so he insisted I abort. After a lot of hesitation, I went ahead with it because I never imagined myself as a single mother, my dream was to have a proper family unit.

It was really sad for me because I had strong feelings for him and would have loved to have his child. This brought about the end of our relationship and it was a really painful time for both of us. I felt I had a deep connection with him and I was very happy in his company but it was difficult because I couldn't see him when I wanted – only when he could free himself. Perhaps his unavailability made him even more attractive to my eyes.

After my father's death, my junior brother Hassan made the choice to become homeless and live in the street even though he had access to my Mum's flat where he had a bed, food and clothes. His life went downhill when one of his most recent girlfriends with whom he had a baby girl decided to end her relationship with him because of his excessive drinking. Instead of straightening his life out, he increased his alcohol intake and added tranquilisers to his daily dose to be able to cope with his depression.

Each time I visited my Mum's home, I heard painful stories about him but was always nervous to see him in person because he was so imposing and intimidating with his tall frame, thick glasses and beard.

When alive, my father was too weak to exercise his authority so instead, my siblings took over this role and got into heavy arguments with Hassan trying to reason with him to stop and get his life cleaned up. All this was in vain. I often wondered if I should have spoken to him myself since my approach and tone was much softer than the rest.

From very young, we learned the only way to get attention in our family was to be the loudest. For example, my youngest brother ended up the tallest, nearly two meters with a protruding belly and a voice that could be heard across a football field!

A couple of years after I left home, Hassan travelled to Algeria with my Mum who arranged for him to marry one of our cousins there. She left him there with his bride who soon became pregnant. Very shortly after, Hassan was back home in France and never returned to Algeria to see his wife or his baby boy. He was obviously unsettled there, a feeling I could totally relate to since life in Algeria was not as comfortable as the one we were used to in France. I don't even know why he agreed to get married there in the first place but maybe the pressure from my Mum was too much for him and he gave in. Anyway, when he got back, he was never the same again, most likely torn with guilt for deserting his pregnant wife. He started a relationship with a French girl and had baby girl with her but soon their relationship soured. He was now living on the street and even more miserable than before. Maybe the alcohol and the tranquilisers, which the family doctor kept prescribing, helped him forget the misery of his life. From my perspective, he was self-destructive and the doctor just let it happen!

One sunny morning as he got drunk, he tripped on the pavement and fell, hitting the back of his head on the ground. He ended up in l'hôpital de Nanterre, in the emergency department in a coma with a brain haemorrhage. He never woke up and passed away within a week, on the 7th August 2001. I just happened to be visiting my Mum that same day and my older brother, Sabir agreed to come and pick me up from the train station. When I asked about Hassan, a question I usually asked when in Paris because I was concerned about him. Sabir paused and said in his calmest tone of voice that Hassan had just died that same morning. I couldn't believe my ears and at first, I thought I misheard. I just sat there astounded not knowing what to say. Was he joking? This brother was a year younger than I, how could this happen? It just didn't make sense.

I couldn't understand why or how even though I knew about his life as a recluse. I felt really bad now not to have spoken to him before, as maybe my words could have helped him. I immediately felt a deep sense of guilt and great sadness, which persisted for a long time to come. I can understand and accept my parents passing away but he was only thirty-seven years old with a long life in front of him.

My poor Mum was absolutely devastated even though he often became aggressive with her and she felt both helpless and afraid when he was around. Now, she had to bury her own son. After many protracted family discussions, it was decided that his body should also be flown back to Algeria and buried next to my Dad's. Similar preparations as for my Dad's funeral were being made for him. I went to the morgue to see his body and say my good bye. This time, I was stronger and didn't need much convincing but it was surreal to see this tall, strong body, lying on the table, lifeless. He was in the prime of life and it was a real tragedy to lose him in this way.

Back in London, many nights I found myself in tears thinking about him and how he decided to let himself go all the way down never to come back up again. I just couldn't understand it. I had so much hope for him. He was the only brother I had with quite a unique entrepreneurial flair. Yet again, this put life into a different perspective for me with so many questions about our mission in this life and what happens after. In the meantime, life was taking its normal course and I was progressing on the career front to where I thought I wanted to be.

I was still living under the same roof as John when I met my next long-term partner, Robert. Robert, originally from Scotland, had been living in London for thirty five years but still kept a slight Glaswegian accent which was quite charming. He was divorced with two lovely young daughters. We met at a Harley Davidson meet up at the famous London Hard Rock Cafe and he chased me for a whole year before I gave in and decided to have a relationship with him. He was the first man I dated who was divorced, much older and had children. Both latter issues were great causes of concern for me. It seemed we had a lot of differences we needed to iron out before we could enjoy a smooth relationship.

In the meantime, I learned to enjoy family life with him when on Saturdays, his daughters came over and we did fun things together like climbing trees and chasing each other in London's beautiful parks, playing games and eating. It was great and he was a very good father to them covering for some of their emotional and financial needs. One of Robert's best qualities was that he managed to maintain and nurture a good friendship with his now happily remarried ex-wife and so making the emotional burden easier on their daughters. They were growing fast though and so were their needs. Every day I was learning how to share my life a bit more with him for unlike John he wasn't putting up with my single mindedness. He also taught me what it was like to have and be part of a family, which was what I eventually wanted one day with the right partner. As we progressed in our relationship, we discussed the subject of starting a family of our own many a time, but he kept hesitating because of his age and he was still helping to raise two daughters already.

I didn't know what to do. I was aware my biological clock was ticking and I wasn't interested in looking for anyone else. I knew that it would take time to meet someone with whom I could develop a relationship and plan a family. Robert was not perfect and neither was I so we often argued and even broke up a few times during our time together but I was confident we could work things out.

My close friends often told me I was wasting my time but I persisted by coming back to him hoping that we could find a mutual agreement. I really enjoyed arriving home after work to someone who very often prepared delicious meals for us to share with a nice bottle of wine. I also loved his high energy level and his boyish craziness, riding his Harley around London often with me as a pillion passenger or taking longs walks in London's famous Hyde Park and Richmond Park.

I regularly travelled to Europe with my work and once a

year, I went on a girls' holiday somewhere in the world with my friend Mariejoe who by now was back in Chile for good - Robert didn't mind.

From the outside, it was all good but deep inside, I wasn't sure about my relationship with him and how far I could go on. Eventually and after many long talks, we tried for a baby for three years before we split up. I never got pregnant with him, raising the question of infertility for one of us at least. Robert had many qualities and had many friends who really liked and appreciated him. He was also extremely resourceful and financially secure which meant I could concentrate on bettering my own career, organising holidays and simply enjoying life with him.

Finally, John, my ex managed to save enough money to put down a deposit on a nice garden flat in North London. Soon we sold our flat in South West London and it was really hard to leave there without a tear in my eyes but deep inside, I knew that it was for the better. When the time came, Robert was kind enough to move John's belongings, which we had split up amicably. As a good friend to John, I even agreed to help him with his credit by putting my name as a guarantor for a bank loan (which the bank refused to give him) which he needed to buy furniture.

The deal was that every month, I would pay a certain amount towards his loan from my bank account and he would transfer the same amount back to mine. Unfortunately, I ended up paying his full loan. He refused to pay me back having being told he had been conned on the flat sale by one of his new lovers, which of course was untrue. As a last solution and before we sold the flat, John proposed to marry me but by then, it was already too late.

We had grown so far apart and Robert was already on the scene. I haven't seen much of John since but last time I saw him he seemed well.

I managed to find a smaller flat in the same area and lived there for only two years as my flat was broken into twice in the space of five months. Even though the flat was really nice,

I never felt safe there again and was spending a lot of time at Robert's home in Central London. Two years later, I sold it and I managed to raise enough money to be able to afford a more secure and cosy flat just opposite beautiful Battersea Park, a street I always wanted to live in. Even though the flat was much smaller, it was central, very well served by buses, trains and taxis and it was an easy, pleasant walk to Chelsea and Knightsbridge from there through the park.

In the meantime, my relationship with Robert was progressing at its own pace and we enjoyed some good times together even travelling to Asia and South Africa. When the time was right for him, he decided to sell his flat in Central London and buy a bigger one nearer his daughters in the hope that he would see them more often now that they were teenagers and had their own lives to lead.

Once he was settled in his new flat, he asked me to move in with him which was a really nice thought but I was upset that he didn't discuss either the purchase nor the location of his new flat with me. It was in a nicer area but more remote. This was a concern for me as it meant I had to depend on him for my night outs during the dark winter season and I didn't feel comfortable with that. At the same time, I was looking for another job as there were major changes at the company I was working for.

Nothing felt really right and I was very hesitant to move in. I wasn't even getting pregnant which would have been a good motivation to encourage the move. I was beginning to get worried about my fertility altogether as I had never carried a pregnancy to term with two abortions. I decided to go for a medical check in case something was wrong and asked him to do the same. Of course, he didn't like the idea and said that already having children proved he was okay. He eventually agreed to go along with the sperm test.

His results were fine and my tests were normal. I couldn't understand what was happening and neither did the doctors so one of the solutions the doctor offered was to have his sperm injected inside my womb as it seemed they never reached their destination - the egg in the fallopian tube. I thought this should be pretty easy and certainly not difficult as nothing appeared wrong with us so I went ahead and made an appointment at the hospital for both of us to go in on a specific day of my cycle. At this point, there was still no commitment for both of us for payment, just our time and day to be there.

When I told Robert what date we should go into hospital together, I was surprised by his reaction when he totally overreacted and refused to go. According to him, it wasn't his problem as he already had two children. Even though I made it clear I was now ready to have a family, he had difficulty seeing me – the career woman and traveller he knew – with a child at home. This was bringing up all sorts of others issues. At first, I was shocked by his strong reaction and his lack of support.

As an escape route, he suddenly started to feel used. In hindsight, I wasn't sure I could live with him without a child as I feared getting in some kind of rut and becoming bored. Having a child was also very important to me in the story of my life. After such a long struggle with my family, I felt the need to leave my legacy so that lessons could be passed on and on, changing the course of the Benzaoui family.

Yes maybe, we were both not very clear about our intentions, he wanted a loving companion with no family responsibility and by now, I wanted a companion and a family – I wanted both. As he stood, stubbornly by his position and I could see he wasn't going to change, I cancelled our appointment at the hospital and decided to end our relationship then and there after 8 years.

What a waste of fertility time was this for me but how much did I learn! I was deeply upset about the situation as this meant abandoning the idea of motherhood, at least in this lifetime. I was now forty five years old, old enough to be a grandmother in today's world.

I needed to move on and think about how I was going to lead my life now, childless with so much energy to spare and so curious about life. I used this time for introspection and with my own stubborn nature, I woke up one day and decided no man was going to be responsible for whether I was going to become a mother or not. After many sleepless nights and endless talks with friends and even strangers at times, I decided ... to go it alone.

Chapter 7

Listen to your convictions,
even if they seem absurd to your reason.

MOTHERHOOD

It was now October 2007 and in November, in my mid-forties, I was finally at peace with the decision to go it alone even though most of my friends thought I was totally mad, irresponsible and most of all selfish. They also strongly believed, in expensive London, I would never be able to raise a child by myself. In the silence of many of my nights, I had that concern too. At this stage though, I was so much into my wish and angry too at finding myself in such a state in my life that I was even prepared to let go of certain judgemental friends to reach my ultimate goal.

It was already difficult to be alone in this and getting criticism was unhelpful for me. Besides, I was already completely aware that I was taking on a huge challenge. So I began researching different clinics in London and overseas which could offer me the best service at a reasonable cost knowing pretty well that choosing this route was going to prove financially and emotionally costly.

I researched clinics showing a high rate of success with women of my age group. If the doctor was right and the sperm was not getting to the eggs, I concluded if I had high quality sperm injected, I should increase my chances of pregnancy. Finally, I found a clinic in Copenhagen which seemed to be very professional and assured me of their high rate of success. I decided to try IUI (Intra Uterine Insemination) with them as they concluded from my test results and my age that was all I needed, for now at least. Really, what was missing in my life was a decent man with whom to do this right now. To complete this procedure, I had to provide the sperm so they recommended a couple of reputable clinics in Denmark where I could buy it, choosing from a number of physical characteristics but not authorised to see any personal information regarding the donor as they were mostly anonymous young students in need of cash who could end up fathering a good number of children around the world.

The clinic I chose was in the centre of Copenhagen and run by a couple of former midwives. Once they had calculated my cycle, they were able to give me the date I needed to travel to them for the little quick procedure which could change my life forever. They also offered the extra option whereby once the child reached the age of eighteen years, he would be able to meet his biological father but only once! I thought I owed this to a child who had never asked to come to this world. At least, he would have seen his biological father. I imagined my child going to meet this father, a much younger person than me and thought how strange the whole situation might be for him. For the next few days, I tried to psyche myself up and prepare for the little intervention I was going to have.

Being a bit at short notice, I booked an expensive day return flight. I had no choice, I had to go on this exact date. It was a very early flight so when the day came in October 2007, I woke up in total darkness, way before sunrise, preparing myself to go by car to the airport - I hate driving in the dark.

That morning, it seemed I was operating in some kind of daze as if still in my dream state, moving mechanically like a robot. I stopped asking myself millions of questions and I was just going for it now. I was ready in good time, waking up at four in the morning, something I normally found quite difficult to do. In that moment, I felt I reached the point of no return and felt completely wrapped up by the surrounding darkness, which reflected the unknown space I was about to step into. I couldn't think anymore. I got into my car and still dazed, drove myself the short way to Heathrow airport. My flight was at 6:45 A.M., which meant I had to be at the airport at 5:30 A.M. at least. It was all so surreal, like a dream or watching someone else acting in a movie. Everything went smoothly and we boarded the

SAS flight 500 at 6 A.M. on the 26th October 2007, destination Copenhagen.

This trip was the result of three months of research and so many unanswered questions. I was now feeling fairly comfortable with the answers I got from the clinic and in consequence, my anxiety was slightly reduced. Who would have thought that one day I would have recourse to such extraordinary services? Just a few years back and still with a lot of internal conflicts, I was considering doing now what was one day, in my mind, the impossible. My life didn't turn out to be what society or even I expected, now I had no choice but to do whatever it took to fulfil a deep desire and longing I had to have a family.

After eight years in a fruitless relationship, I was left with no option but to go it alone, completely against my moral belief of never wanting to be a single mother.

Since this was going to be a quick procedure taking less than two hours to complete, I was returning home on the same day. I was happy with the thought of being back in my nice big bed and my lovely warm and cosy flat in South West London. The flight went smoothly and I was reading passages of the book, *Feel the Fear and Do it Anyway* by Louise Hay, which I found very inspirational in crucial moments like these. The flight was half empty at that hour which meant I could focus on myself for the duration of the flight. We landed in Copenhagen in good time.

I found the clinic in the centre and even had time to go to *Katz coffee shop* nearby for breakfast before the clinic opened. I was their first appointment giving them plenty of time so I could make my flight back to London. As my appointment time approached, I was very aware of my heart beating faster than usual. I wasn't having second thoughts but I was becoming aware of the magnitude of the possible consequences of what I was about to undertake if it succeeded. Was I really mad? Whilst a few of my friends who knew about such things thought so, I didn't.

I thought about the time in my mid-thirties when I was briefly pregnant, but I just wasn't prepared to raise a child and with no enthusiasm from my partner, I simply wasn't strong enough to go it alone. But now, I knew in my heart that I was ready and this was my chosen path.

I took a few yoga-style deep breaths to help calm my spirit and walked the few steps from the coffee shop to the clinic. At first, the white building looked like a block of luxury apartments but there were mostly offices in there and the clinic *Vitanova* was on the second floor. Once inside, the clinic was spacious, airy, all painted in white giving it a clean, medical look. I could sense a certain peaceful energy about the place and I slowly started to relax.

The nurses' voices were soft and calming music was playing in the background. I introduced myself to the receptionist who was expecting me. She kindly asked me to sit on a white leather sofa across the room, just like the one I have in my own lounge. I decided to dress trendy, warm and comfortably so I wore a short white skirt with black high boots and I felt really good about myself. I sat quietly and waited for my turn to come.

As I was sitting there trying not to look inward by concentrating my mind on the women's magazine I was flicking through, the treatment room opened and two ladies came out followed by a little happy toddler. It was a beautiful picture and I concluded that these ladies were a lesbian couple here to be inseminated with their second child. It gave me hope to see that at least their first attempt worked and there was this lovely little boy of no more than two years old walking right behind them. I smiled within and relaxed further.

Then my turn came. Hannah, the nurse in charge came to sit next to me in the waiting room and offered me a glass of water, which I gladly accepted. She kept smiling and didn't say much as she was trying to get a feel for my level of anxiety before taking me to the treatment room. She asked me a few questions and then asked me to follow her in. It was a spacious white room with what looked like a risen queen size bed and it had a stool at its foot. In her very calm voice, she explained the procedure to me and showed the catheter she was going to use to inject the sperm into my uterus. All she asked me to do is to keep calm and relaxed with my legs wide open in front of her whilst she was sitting on the stool to do her job.

From what she has asked me earlier, she was confident I knew what I was doing; otherwise she said she had the right to refuse treatment. She was also very surprised to see that I looked so much younger than my age as it was our first and hopefully last meeting.

Her observations made me smile because this wasn't the first time I heard such compliments from people and every time that happened, I thanked my parents for their good genes. She went out of the room for a few minutes to thaw and prepare the sperm I bought. At the same time, a lovely lady acupuncturist came in to put some needles in appropriate meridian points on my body to help relax my nerves and prepare my body for the treatment.

My acupuncture session was over after thirty minutes; Hannah came back to the room. She asked me to lie down on the bed with my legs wide open facing the stool. I did so, feeling totally vulnerable in this position.

She used cold metal callipers to open the entrance to my vagina so she could insert the catheter through my cervix as far in as possible making the journey to the ovaries dramatically shorter. Once she felt she got there, she pushed the liquid out and all I could feel was a slight pressure in the lower part of my abdomen. She removed the catheter from inside me and asked me to lie on the bed and relax. She kept eye contact with me throughout the treatment reassuring me and guiding me through what she was doing. She then proceeded to call the acupuncturist again to complete her treatment, placing needles on the same points as before for a few minutes. Apparently, research showed that acupuncture helps relax the system and so increases the chances of getting pregnant.

I couldn't believe it was done. I was thrilled at the thought that it could work and I didn't need to have a man physically with me to get pregnant, just money was enough for now. I was tired of relying on the male gender for my emotional fulfilments. This lovely Danish lady put the needles accordingly and left me to relax on the big bed in this white room with my feet up. Everything still seemed so surreal. I guess I was still wondering what was happening to me and dozed off for a few minutes and before I knew it she had returned.

Now she removed the needles very gently, one by one and when she was done, wished not to see me again for good luck then left. After a few minutes, I stood up and adjusted my clothes. I was ready to leave and make my way back to the airport to catch my flight home to London where my life was right now. I was feeling a little light-headed but soon that passed. I came out of the room and went to reception to sort out my bill. The nurses all wished me the best of luck and suddenly, I was in the street again as if nothing had happened.

Unbelievable! It was that easy but there was no guarantee this method would work first time.

I reached the airport in plenty of time again and felt like I was walking on air, nothing around me seemed to bother me and it was like I was invisible to the world, totally wrapped up in my own cocoon and feeling confident about what I had just done and about the future. It was an exhilarating feeling and in a strange way, so empowering.

The flight was nice and very peaceful. I reached home in the early evening safely and decided to pamper myself that evening. I prepared a nice hot bath with my preferred bath oils and candles accompanied by soft music in the background which helped me drift off where I imagined myself lying on a sunny beach with turquoise coloured water and beautiful golden sand. This amazing scenery I hold close to my heart especially when around me, life gets chaotic. In this case, I just felt so relaxed, warm and content. I got ready for bed and cuddled up in my nice warm duvet with a big smile on my face. That night, I slept like a baby completely unaware of what was happening inside my womb.

I woke up refreshed and happy, ready for a good day ahead. At that time, I was working from home so I set myself up and started to make phone calls to my customers in Western Europe. Up to now, I was feeling nothing different in my womb and it felt like I hadn't done anything. I called my friend Mariejoe in Chile who knew what I did and shared my experience with her. She was thrilled for me even though she thought I was a little mad. She made me promise her that I was going to just relax at home that day and look after myself not returning immediately to my crazy, active lifestyle.

She knew I liked to be out and about doing one thing or another having such a hyperactive personality, which seemed to run in our family. However, I felt so good the next day that I decided to go to my ceroc dance class (modern jive) that evening where I was sure to have fun, completely ignoring her wise advice. I finished my work day, got ready, wore my best dance outfit with my comfortable dance shoes and off I went. I arranged to meet up with one of my dance friends there and danced non-stop until 11 P.M.

I was feeling so good and so light that my dance partners picked up on this energy. They either gave me a big hug or a kiss on the cheek after each dance with them, which was fairly unusual. There was definitely something different in the air. I was trying to stay connected with my inner body to try and feel what was happening inside and was dancing slower than usual. I felt so happy having had so much fun, went home to get ready for a good night sleep, totally satisfied with my night out.

The next day, I decided to just relax as I was going to be travelling to Europe for work the week after. This was a regular activity in my profession and to be honest, I was beginning to tire of it. Mariejoe called me to get some news and got pretty upset when I told her I went out dancing the night before. She thought it was irresponsible and that I wasn't giving my body the time to do its work As I had never done this before and never took The Pill in my life, I thought we saw each other regularly I had all the chances in the world for this to work so I didn't worry about her opinion. A part of me was a little terrified at the prospect this could work but I preferred not to think about it and carried on with my daily chores and relaxing times like walking in the beautiful Battersea Park right across my from home.

On the third day though, I started to get slightly worried because I could feel absolutely no activity in my abdomen or breasts. If my first attempt didn't work, my period was due in the next two days. I felt absolutely fine physically but then one day I noticed a little blood in my panty and I nearly fainted with despair. The treatment didn't work and I was absolutely devastated. I was healthy and fit even for my age – why didn't it work? I was confused and couldn't understand.

I was in tears now and immediately called the clinic to ask what I should do next. They were sorry to hear my news and could only tell me that sometimes with this treatment, a woman has to try at least five times. I was surprised as they didn't mention this before, there was no way I could afford to pay for multiple treatments plus all the travel expenses and the time off from work. I was really so disappointed and started to realise that after all, maybe I couldn't control everything in my life. Because of my biological age, they recommended I try again but also said that I might have better chances of success with IVF (In Vitro Fertilization). IVF is an even more invasive treatment than IUI and a lot more expensive. They recommended a clinic in another part of Denmark if I wished to go for this treatment.

I thought about it for a few days and I decided to give IUI another try in the next month's cycle which was due in November 2007. During that month, I was also turning forty five years of age and suddenly realised I may have missed the boat completely. I had been single for five months now and felt I was taking charge of my life doing the treatments without leaving motherhood to the chance of meeting a decent man in the immediate future. I soon was to realise the meaning of the word destiny when things didn't turn out the way I wanted them to.

I was out for my birthday drink with friends and was having a good time although still a bit shocked by the recent result of my first medical attempt to get pregnant. I danced and drank champagne until the early hours of the morning mostly sharing the dance floor with a young man called David who was a friend of one my friends there. He wasn't at all my type but I was attracted to the fact that he moved beautifully and rhythmically on the dance floor. We danced together until the bar closed and I invited him back to mine for a drink.

David was a fairly young man still "searching for himself" regularly using highly toxic stimulants like cigarettes, alcohol, and more, to feel comfortable in social situations. With him in my intimate life now, I cancelled my appointment for my second IUI as I wanted to give myself a chance with him.

The first time I went out for dinner with David, a friend of mine who saw us made an interesting comment and asked if I was spoon-feeding him as he acted so shy and unsure of himself. This made me wonder what I was doing with him myself. Yes, David was young and virile but he was also a smoker and a drinker. What was I doing again? From the onset, there was no chance for this relationship to work but it gave me hope that maybe I could still get pregnant and finally have a family. It seems I was doing this at any cost now as time for sure was not on my side.

Soon enough, we started a relationship and we saw each regularly which was quite nice as he was a very smart man and we could talk about anything, even better after a few drinks. Soon, he made it clear he wanted more than a relationship with me but noticed every time he spoke seriously like this, he was often too drunk to remember his words the next day. We were not using any protection and so there was always a chance I could get pregnant if my body and spirit desired it.

In the meantime, I went to see a doctor in London to get an explanation as to why I wasn't getting pregnant other than my age. He recommended I had a laparoscopy to check if there was something wrong in the womb or if the tubes were blocked. So I was admitted to hospital for an overnight stay in February 2008. I didn't tell David the exact reason why I was in hospital.

He was around and checking on me but I was beginning to realise he was unable to give himself emotionally as he was so scared, inexperienced and emotionally immature. If I had attracted such a person in my life right now when all I needed was a solid relationship, was I yet again, sabotaging my last chance to reach my goal? And if this was true, why did I keep doing this? Nothing was clear in my head anymore. This relationship was so much hard work already and not worth it right now. Did I really and honestly want this child in my life or was I too scared of the responsibility or the life change it entailed? I had so many questions and no answers.

One day, I decided to have an honest discussion with David to confirm how serious he was about wanting a family with me, he had expressed this on one of those drunken evenings, losing his inhibitions and able to express himself openly. But more importantly, did I want a family with him? So I took courage and decided to initiate such a chat with him at my own risk having no idea what his reaction could be. The next thing I remember, he was running out of the door as far away from me as possible. It all took him by surprise and he got into such a panic when he heard I wasn't on the pill, even though I had told him once before when he asked me - but he had no recollection of this, of course.

I was a little shaken at this point realising everything we had discussed when he was drunk, had not been consciously registered by his hazy brain. Now I didn't know anymore who I was with, this very lively drunk boyfriend or the quiet and shy man of the day after. I was so confused and wanted out of this.

Soon after realising yet again, I didn't have a future with him, I decided to take my fate in my hands once again, and continue the IVF route especially since the results of my recent laparoscopy didn't show any anomalies.

I contacted an infertility clinic in Denmark as I had many questions to ask them before making my final decision. This was such a big step for me both financially and emotionally and I was so nervous. I consulted with two of my closest friends again who still thought I was totally mad but appreciated the way I stuck to my wish. I needed someone close to me to know what I was doing just in case I did turn a bit mad. In the meantime, I reconciled with David and although he was still around me, I chose not to share this part of my life with him as it was a very delicate and difficult time for me. After all, it was my life, my responsibility and my money.

It was in June 2008, I decided to go for my next treatment.

Once I was clear about what the process involved, the timing, the medication including the injections, and more importantly their rate of success for women in my age group, I agreed to make an appointment with the doctor who was coordinating the whole process from London. His duty was to follow my treatment and supply me with the medication until I was ready to go to Denmark. Dr. Onwude was a really nice man specialising in infertility. Although his cost was not part of my budget, after meeting him in person and he explained the procedure to me step by step, I was happy to pay for his services. He was so reassuring. He was going to prescribe and supply all the medication needed to stimulate ovulation, do the scanning to see how many eggs were there and monitor their size until such time when they were ready to be aspirated and fertilised with the sperm I bought once again. One of the drugs to stimulate the ovaries was an injection I had to do myself around my belly button for a few days. It was odd at first, I thought I couldn't do that to myself but quickly, I got used to it. I had the image in my head of a drug addict injecting herself with drugs, something I never did nor will do in my life.

In the meantime, the same questions were bombarding my little head, it was mind blowing. Was I doing the right thing? Was it selfish of me to choose such a route? Was I thinking about the child's welfare? Would I be able to cope? What if I ended up with twins? What if the child was born with a handicap? Would I have enough money to raise the child by myself? Would I be a good mother? Would I be able to love my child? Sometimes, I hesitated and other times, I had such moments of clarity that deep inside myself, I was certain I was doing the right thing. A couple of my closest friends were following this process and it was nice to have this support as this was such an enormous decision for me.

I kept it quiet from everyone else as I didn't want to have to defend myself against those friends of mine who disagreed with my actions. At this stage, I needed to gather and conserve my inner strength to be able to cope with what was coming next.

At the time of my first IVF treatment, I was between two jobs so I didn't have to worry about taking time off and I could just relax and concentrate on myself for a change. During the medication process, everything seemed to be going according to plan and the eggs were growing steadily. I was getting more and more excited about the prospect that this could work as it definitely had more chances of success than the IUI. For once too, I felt the money spent on medication and Dr Onwude's consultations and scans was money well spent.

Around me, people kept saying that there was a certain glow about me and I felt excited once again not to have to rely on a relationship with a man for this to happen. Yes, David was still around but the relationship was going absolutely nowhere. We gave each other the affection we needed when we needed it trying desperately not to get attached to any emotions that came with it. I was feeling so happy, excited and hopeful. I shared parts of my treatment with my younger sister Alima with whom I always felt a special connection. She was fairly open to the idea but I am sure she also thought I was totally out of my mind to try and get pregnant at my age without being in a solid relationship. She herself was twice married and raising three children at the time.

I sounded out some of my male friends about the subject of IVF, though I didn't tell them that it was something I was going through. Most of them thought it was crazy and selfish. Normally, that kind of reaction would have shaken me but now it didn't. I felt that I was stronger now in my convictions than ever and more sure that my body was up to the challenge.

Even Dr Onwude who was coordinating with my doctor in Denmark seemed to be quite happy with how I was responding to medication considering my age.

After a couple of scans, he was satisfied that in a few days, I would be able to fly to Denmark for my treatment. This time, I organised myself in advance and bought a flight ticket on the dates indicated by Dr. Karsten in Denmark so I got my flight ticket at a reasonable price. But again, as the time drew near I had mixed feelings, half excited and half nervous. In a way, I was constantly aware of an internal unconscious conflict having reached this stage of my life still to become a single mother! I never wanted to be that and it was the main reason for having aborted twice in my life.

At the same time, through friends, I made contact with other women who were going through the same process as well and had succeeded after the second or third attempts. I so envied their courage and determination. Usually, those were women in high powered jobs that seemed to have supportive families around them so once their babies were born, the family stepped in to help out in the absence of a father. This seemed to be an increasing trend in today's society with women becoming financially independent, spending too much time at work and no time to meet the right partner.

Unfortunately, the female biological clock seems to be ticking faster than we wish and by the time we wake up to reality, it is already too late. I found that people are were still arguing that no single women should be allowed to have IVF treatment as it is immoral and could be interpreted as selfish and irresponsible.

Results show so far though, apart from the increased risk of giving birth to more than one child, the children born out of those treatments are perfectly balanced emotionally and healthy. And more often than not, they soon end up having a step father who takes on the role of their biological father perfectly. The other solution for women these days is to freeze their eggs until such time they finally meet the partner with whom they want a family. That way, they are attempting to preserve the quality of the eggs even though it still remains an expensive avenue.

A couple of weeks into the treatment, my eggs were nearly ready to be released for fertilization and Dr Karsten gave me a date to come in for my treatment. The good news was at least, I did have eggs so something so far was working properly. I was told some women much younger than I didn't produce any eggs not even with the help of medication. They seemed to have none left.

A woman is born with roughly one to two million eggs or

follicles and about a thousand of them are released every month until she hasn't got anymore left. When a woman reaches puberty, only four hundred thousands of them remain. Each month after that time, only one egg is released and is picked up by the fallopian tube. If there is sexual intercourse at this time, fertilization may take place. It sounds like a real game of luck to me. This means that only four hundred eggs will ever mature. With age though, the supply of eggs declines and once this supply is depleted, menstruation ends completely and it is menopause time.

It was a beautiful, hot June in London and I was all ready to travel to Denmark when to my pleasant surprise, my good friend Adele decided to join me on this trip wanting to film the procedure for a possible future documentary. I agreed she could do that and I felt better for having her with me too as I was getting really nervous. I also really enjoyed the support of Dr Onwude who was very promising as to the results. I was excited and felt wonderful.

Just before the trip, the scan showed eight follicles out of which four were bigger and most probably would be the ones the clinic would use for fertilization. It wasn't many but as it was explained to me, it was quality that counted right now not quantity, especially at my age.

In my life plan, I regularly saved money for the education of my unborn child. Now I was allowing myself to use part of this money to give birth to this child first before it could get an education. Even though I was going through the treatment smoothly without any side effects at all, all sorts of thoughts were going through my mind. What if the treatment worked? What if it didn't? Would I be able to meet a decent man with whom to share the rest of my life? Will I die alone? I had so many questions going through my head and not one answer. If the treatment worked, it would definitely define the rest of my life, spent raising this so wanted child who would be my immediate family and part of me. I felt strange to find myself in this situation, once again fighting for what I wanted most not even being able to think about the consequences and possible pregnancy complications at all.

But if the treatment didn't work by January 2009, I would make the world my own and take off to do everything which I held back on while waiting for motherhood. Also, if it didn't work, I would have the rest of my life to find my life partner if I wanted to, now that the procreation pressure was off, I could at least enjoy the journey.

Simply enjoying life for what it is was slowly becoming my new motto. For example, David was for the moment, there were too many issues in the relationship and I felt I didn't want to spend my time sorting someone else's problems on top of all those that I was battling with. Instead, I wanted a partner with whom I could share my life and do things with.

Despite my strong feelings for him, I wasn't figuring him into my future at all and that was a positive sign. I felt more at peace now, I started to spend money on trying to make up for some of the bad decisions I made in my past, like staying far too long in the wrong relationships. At least now I know that even if it didn't work, I had given it a real chance.

So, here I was in Denmark waiting for the next day to go back to the clinic for them to put at least two fertilised eggs back into my womb. I was a bit disappointed that the clinic didn't call me to let me know how many eggs had actually fertilized out of the five follicles they took out. It was such a slow and microscopic process that maybe they couldn't tell until at least seventy-two hours had passed. I was secretly hoping more than two were fertilised so that I could freeze a couple to use in a future cycle if this one failed.

Their objective was to put back two fertilised eggs, which was the legal limit in Denmark. Of course, this increased the risk of multiple pregnancies but also gave an extra chance in case one didn't survive.

Technology is just so amazing and my research showed this clinic was particularly successful with older women. They didn't treat women over the age of forty-six years old because the percentage of positive results after that age was just not worth the effort or expense. I was just a few months away from this age, desperately racing against time!

It was so good to have Adele with me and in fact, she distracted me from the very real reason we were there for and I really enjoyed her company. The next day, we got ready and took a taxi back to the clinic where doctor and nurses were waiting for me.

I was very nervous about the possible discomfort but they had told me that removing the follicles was the most uncomfortable part of the whole process. Today should be quick and easy. It all still felt a bit surreal for me and whilst I was going through the procedure I couldn't really believe what I was doing. Adele's presence and voice was my confirmation I wasn't dreaming.

Once I was ready to receive the eggs, the doctor coordinated with the nurse in charge who was in the next room where the incubator was. She had to quickly get the eggs into the catheter, pass them through a connecting window to the doctor who was then going to insert the micro-tube inside my uterus and release the fertilized eggs.

Before they started this process though, they informed me that out of the five follicles removed yesterday only two became fertilised. Only one of those was of good quality; one had two cells and the other, four.

They asked me how many eggs I wanted back in me and my first answer was one only. I had a vision of twins and started panicking. I didn't even know if I was able to cope with one child single-handed let alone two. Normally, this procedure recommends two eggs be put back to increase one's chances of success. So after explaining to me the pros and cons of having two eggs back in and seeing how reluctant I was, I became confused and dazed for a few minutes. In the end, I agreed the two should be put back. This also meant if I needed to try another cycle, I needed to go through the whole procedure again because there were no eggs of good quality that could be frozen for future use.

I nervously watched the staff prepare the eggs ready for insertion, I was now at the point of no return.

Dr Petersen switched the camera on so we could see the

microscopic dots of eggs. It was just absolutely incredible. He pushed the catheter in and I didn't even feel anything. It was done in a matter of seconds and I was ready to leave the clinic now patiently waiting for the results in the next few days. Adele was with me in the room filming the whole procedure.

What if it worked? What if it didn't work? Once more, those questions kept flashing back and forth in my mind. I would know in no less than two weeks' time when my period was due. I felt an incredible sense of liberation and lightness and felt like rejoicing, a heavy weight had been lifted off my shoulders. I had pushed my boundaries even further and expanded my comfort zones so much and actually felt physically larger! Whatever the result, my life was changing forever with or without the child.

Rest and meditation were the two activities on my agenda for the next few days until the start of my new job. We arrived back in London safely and I left Adele at Victoria Station whilst I made my way home to Battersea Park still wrapped up in this veil of peace. Once in, I took a hot bath with relaxing oils and slept a very sound and deep sleep.

That June 2008, my two sisters and I were going to Egypt on a Nile cruise to celebrate Farida's fiftieth birthday. The trip was organised from Paris so I had to make my way to Paris airport to join my sisters there for our flight to Luxor where the cruise began. After four days at home packing, I travelled to Paris to join them for the flight.

I was feeling fine as if nothing was happening inside me. My sisters vaguely understood what I had just gone through and I didn't really feel like explaining details. So far, other than Adele, I shared this with my two closest friends, Jeanette and Mariejoe.

I reached Paris safely and waited for my sisters at Charles De Gaulle Airport but arrived so far ahead of time that the wait seemed like an eternity. We were flying at night-time and would land at Luxor at 5 A.M. the next day.

Whilst at the airport, I started to feel a little discomfort in my lower abdomen having just spent eight hours sitting on the bus from London to Paris. I was slightly concerned that I was about to sit for another five hours on the flight to Luxor.

My energy was soft and loving as I received so much love from my friends and David who was not aware of what I had just gone through. In the last few days, I was playing relationship counsellor to two of my lovely friends trying to help them see their respective situations more clearly. I myself still had so much to learn about relationships with the other sex. Problems in relationships often seem to stem from a serious lack of communication.

In the meantime, Dr Onwude was quite impressed with my treatment and was hopeful for a positive result. It was done now and for now, I was going to enjoy my holidays with my sisters, it was the first trip we took together in our whole lives. I was very curious to see how we would get on together as we are so very different. My sisters have such *joie de vivre* and like to have a good laugh whenever they could.

The flight went smoothly and for most of it, we all slept. When we arrived, I was excited that my sisters were discovering Egypt for the first time. I had travelled to Egypt a few times for business and twice for pleasure. Although I knew that culturally, we weren't interested in the same things, I knew they would have a good time there.

Once we boarded our ship, I made sure Farida was installed in a deluxe room with a double bed as part of her birthday treat whilst Alima and I shared a twin room on the same deck. The idea was to sleep and take all our meals on the ship and spend the daytime visiting different temples scattered along the Nile.

I had informed our tour guide of Farida's birthday so the chef could prepare a special dinner. When her day came, the celebration totally took her by surprise, she never expected so much attention. The chef baked a special cake for her, decorated with her name. It was so nice to see the whole dining room lit up with singing and dancing to Arabic music. She just couldn't believe her eyes. She said later it was the best birthday she ever had. We were so thrilled for her.

As we cruised along, we admired the breathtaking views on both sides of the Nile with all its history and awesome beauty. We enjoyed chatting to the French people with whom we shared our table and finding out about their lives. Generally, all the guests were friendly and relaxed.

On our ship, there happened to be a group of mentally handicapped people whom immediately reminded us of our brother Nasser with Down's Syndrome and we quickly felt very comfortable with them even though some other people were less tolerant of the slight disruption they sometimes brought to this peaceful setting. It was nice to see they too were having a good time, sometimes dancing with us after dinner.

I enjoyed the cultural visits we did on a daily basis and I was learning more about Egypt even though I had been on a Nile cruise the previous year with my ex-boyfriend. It was quite interesting finding out about Hatshepsut, a powerful female pharaoh who reigned for a long time in Egypt.

As I was hoping, my sisters really had an enjoyable time. They laughed, danced, sang and made new friends. Most of all, they enjoyed a well-earned rest from their busy lives in Paris. As for me, I was feeling okay just uncomfortable at times in my lower abdomen not knowing what was going on down there. The week indeed had passed so quickly and the day came when we had to pack our bags and fly back to Paris. It was another tiring night flight but it went smoothly and everyone was happy.

I stayed with my sister Farida in Nanterre whilst Alima's husband came to pick her up in the afternoon to take her back home where her children were waiting for her. In the early evening, as I was relaxing to get ready for bed, I visited the toilet and was horrified when I saw bloodstains in my panty.

Of course, my first impulse was to scream out loud so the whole world would hear me. My despair was so vast and I immediately wondered why life was so unfair.

Instead, I had no choice but to control my feelings and so many tears began to flow out as I could feel my deep pain coming through the core of my being. I tried to reason with myself. It wasn't happening for me and I couldn't understand why, especially when the treatment went so very well and I was a reasonably fit woman.

In this moment, I felt totally powerless and didn't know what to do. This was totally out of my hands once again. I began to wonder what all this meant and for once, I seriously began to doubt myself and the process I was going through. Maybe my subconscious was stopping the success of the process that consciously, I wanted so much. I couldn't share this with Farida yet, the only person around me at the time so instead I withdrew into myself until I was due to return to London a couple of days after.

I had no choice but to learn to accept life as it was, without a child and started to look at all the possibilities the situation opened up. Though, I couldn't help thinking life was so unfair especially when children were born to those young women who couldn't even take care of themselves and needed the government's help - using our tax money.

I returned to my home in London where I roamed aimlessly for a few days coming to terms with what had just happened. I had the urge now to go and explore the world and do things. I wanted to work in an orphanage in Chile, go to India to certify as a yoga teacher, live in a warm climate, learn guitar again and take more dance lessons. All of a sudden, life prospects became so exciting! Should I even consider adopting a child? Who knows what life had in store for me? Only time would tell and reveal the direction I should take.

Whilst all this was going on in my head, I called the clinic to inform them of my bad news. The doctor could not explain what happened but he thought most probably it was a problem with implantation. Of course, they were really disappointed because my failure also affected their success-rate statistics.

It was now June 2008 and in five months' time, I would turn forty-six and no longer be eligible for treatment. Of course, they asked me to consider having another attempt and said I would think about it. It was quite tempting, but the expense was what was holding me back.

I took the time to speak with my sister Alima and two of my friends about the decision to try again. I came to the decision that this was the biggest thing that I would ever do in my life and that should give it every chance possible. I would do it, I would try one last time.

My life was back to normal for now and I still was with David even though with time, it was becoming clearer we had nothing in common. Yet I kept seeing him. My experience with David helped me discover I was able to love unconditionally and it was wonderful that I felt so at one with him.

Now I made my decision, the time for my next treatment was approaching fast and I needed to get ready psychologically and financially for this even though there were still absolutely no guarantees of success.

The problem with implantation was apparently fairly common with women above the age of forty, 'just keep trying' they said.

I still needed to keep my hopes fairly high and hold out hope a little longer. I felt that if a second cycle failed, adoption should be my last option. That little girl from Chile would do me well. One to whom I could give a better life opportunity. Even after having all these nice thoughts in my head, I was still feeling rather low. Dr Onwude told me this was normal after taking the drugs to stimulate my hormones. Anyway, I was not giving up just so I gathered strength for my treatment which was due in August, two months after starting my new job.

In the meantime, my relationship with David was deteriorating and I decided to let it go as I had to concentrate on myself first. We were living such different lives. Now that I was getting stronger, I could see the situation more clearly, it was less painful to come out of it. I needed someone who could be a part of my family, looking after and caring for each other.

In the meantime, I was so excited to start my new job. Although it was the smallest company I ever worked for, I liked the natural toiletries products they created and the packaging that went with them. For me this job also meant no more travelling to the Continent, a four-day week, and a very short drive to work. It was ideal. This way I could improve my social life, my relationships and I could do some work on myself, cook and entertain my friends.

I was ready to explore the emotional side of myself in more

depth; something I could never do before. It seemed like a daunting task at first but the difference now was I wasn't afraid to get in there anymore. I was getting a bit tired of approaching every situation in my life as if it was a business situation completely devoid of emotion and full of ego. In fact, I wasn't even sure I was able to feel any emotions anymore. I needed to find myself within again as I knew most answers came from there once I was able to leave the busy commotion of the mind behind and entered into the silence of my heart.

It was now August 2008 and I found myself in Denmark one more time and alone this time. I was much more confident and clear about what I wanted and felt really good about it. Like my previous experience, everything went well whilst I was taking the medication at home with no side effects at all. As usual, Dr Onwude was very pleased with the result of both scans his nurse did on me. Apparently, there were more eggs this time thus increasing the chances of fertilization and possibility of freezing a few if necessary.

To my great surprise, they aspirated thirteen follicles, more than what the scan showed in the last two days. I didn't think I had so many left although unlike my previous experience, I did feel a little tired and nauseated for a few days before as my ovaries were overworking. I slept a lot once the aspiration was done, which was good and everything was fine.

When I went to the clinic the next day to have the eggs put back, they informed me that actually only two had fertilised and they were of better quality than last time. I was disappointed though there weren't enough for freezing. Let's see if this time they live inside me and decide to cling to life. However, the aspiration of so many follicles left me with severe discomfort in my lower abdomen.

That day, I felt I was relying even less on men in my life no longer being in a relationship. However, I did meet another man in the meantime but he seemed to be worse than David so I decided not to continue seeing him as I didn't want to waste anymore of my precious time with the wrong person, something I was really good at. My choice of men was getting worse as I seemed to be attracting the opposite of what I needed. Mostly, they were very smart, smokers, rebels and emotionally unavailable. There was no possible future with them whatsoever.

Now that I was familiar with the procedure at the clinic I was not nervous, I was just going through the motions until it was completed. Once done, I was ready to go back home but this time round, waiting for the late flight felt so long. I managed to use my alone time to focus within, read and meditate. Flying so late meant I would be in bed by two in the morning but I was sure all this was worth both money and time. I was not thinking of anything else right now other than waiting to see if the treatment succeeded this time. Depending on the results I was confident sensing where to take my life next. I felt so grateful for the many good things life offered me so far and for everything else just waiting to unfold right in front of me soon. Suddenly, life became exciting again.

Back in London, I quickly went back to my routine as if nothing happened. I wasn't sure what was happening inside but I was feeling more uncomfortable than last time. I was also feeling depressed but needed to keep going and move through this phase knowing pretty sure my path would reveal itself soon enough. I remembered feeling the same when I was in Egypt; not being my usual happy self after the treatment but they explained the medication had something to do with it. I needed to stay focussed as a new phase was starting, with or without a child: writing my book, working in a charity shop, learning acupressure, guitar, and so on. To fill up my home, I even considered adopting a cat. Right now, feeling life was fascinating and full of surprises, I totally trusted the process to be able to come out on the other side intact with no deep scars. Now I had two attempts at the treatment, I felt even more at peace within.

A few days later, it felt like even less was happening inside me and I had none of the symptoms I experienced last time round. What was going on? I couldn't do anything. I just had to wait as I had absolutely no power to control nature. They say life carries on no matter what happens. I kept myself busy because when I stopped I cried. My swollen tummy was now flat again and not hurting anymore. I was even back into my yoga and dance classes routine which I totally enjoyed. It was now just a question of time, waiting to see the result.

This time, my period was only one day late but there was no mistake, it came. A deep red colour like I hadn't seen before. At first, I sat in shock and all sorts of questions rushed to my mind. What now? Where do I go from here? Was this possible and if so why hasn't the treatment worked again? I terminated two relationships trying to focus on my goal and now even this was not working. I was at a loss not knowing what to do anymore. I just stayed there motionless as if paralysed not knowing what I was supposed to feel, say, or do. All those years, I kept myself sane, fit, and saving money just in case I was going to raise a family with my partner and now it looked like it would never happen. I had another twenty-five years of good health ahead of me and decided to dedicate it to my unborn child and family. At least this was my plan but it seemed life had something else in store for me.

It was odd but at this point, I felt both devastated and relieved and until today I still can't explain why I felt this way. A part of me was probably just happy to have such a big burden off my shoulders, getting on with my life without any guilt for not having a family because at least I tried. I was a bit confused though about whether I should have another go or not as the clinic kept reminding me they couldn't treat me anymore past November when I turned forty six. That was in two months from now and maybe my last chance.

Deep inside and from the beginning, I always felt what I was doing was wrong. I was torn between my beliefs and my biological clock. My dream, like many women's dreams was to have a family unit. Now that I was at the end of my fertility years, I was considering bringing a child to this earth all by myself and without a father. What happened to my dream? What happened to my morals? Did I get lost on the way? I couldn't think anymore.

Many of my friends considered my desire for a child utterly selfish and other ones completely approved. Like me they were watching me, waiting for the results.

It is really difficult to judge what someone else is doing unless you put yourself in their shoes, unless you walk their walk. Everyone comes from different backgrounds, circumstances, and life stories. The most important thing was what I believed was the right thing for me to do right then in my life. I question until today still the abortion I had at age thirty-five because I couldn't imagine myself as a single mother. At that time, I didn't feel strong enough to raise a child by myself but in hindsight, I would have done a better job than certain people on this planet. Had I known then what I know now, I would have decided otherwise and gone ahead with the pregnancy. I regretted this decision.

Adoption was my last option but other than offering this child the life he or she would never have had otherwise, I wanted a child who was also part of me, my legacy. I needed to learn to accept my life just the way it was now and began to be excited about the prospect of meeting a potential partner who would unconditionally love me, look after me, and spoil me. I was giving up the fight and was ready to enjoy every day with my family and my friends. Limitless possibilities suddenly opened up in front of me. That day, I met up with a friend who knew nothing about the treatment and went for a very long walk by the river Thames with her chatting about many other life subjects. I felt totally at one and at peace with myself and thought that after all, life is not that bad.

After the August failed attempt, I carried on leading a normal life and actually felt better about many things. I thought deeply and wisely and decided actually to have a last attempt in October to complete my time with the clinic in Denmark as after that date, I couldn't go back to them. I was preparing for the treatment once again, looking after myself, eating well, and not drinking alcohol. There was no explanation for the problem of implantation, not even from the doctors so I couldn't do anything more to improve the results. In the meantime, work was going very well and I was enjoying my four days a week in my small office in Balham. The economic situation in the UK at the time hit rock bottom.

So many businesses were reluctant to spend money and take on new products to sell in their shops but it was my job to make sure they did. They did and I quickly started to make up for the lower salary I was getting earning good commissions.

It was now September 2008, and for no particular reason other than trying to pull away from him, I didn't hear from David for a little while and missed him. One night really late, he finally turned up at my door step, drunk again, to declare his love to me. He left after that and that was it. I had no news from him until I went for my treatment in October. Of course, I was a bit confused and was left in the dark as to what exactly he wanted from me. I wasn't sure what I expected but somehow his visit raised my hopes that perhaps we could give the relationship another go. At least I was ready for that and I thought he was too! I was wrong once again. I got into a habit of always finding excuses for his behaviour. All I wanted was to be able to detach from him emotionally so at least I could enjoy the beautiful moments we spent together. Life was getting shorter and no one was allowed to come into mine to distract my inner peace, which I constantly was trying to protect from negative energies and worked on for years. Joy is everywhere one wants to see it and feel it, just like the sun is available for everyone to feel.

In the meantime, a couple of quite disturbing incidents happened. I decided to get a cat from Battersea Dogs Home where they do an amazing job collecting abandoned pets, looking after them and finding new homes for them. I saw the cat I liked and arranged for a member of staff to come and check if my flat was fit to receive such a pet. After the interview at my home, I received a letter from them saying that unfortunately they could not give me the cat because my lifestyle was not suitable. They thought the cat needed to have someone more present at home to play with it. I couldn't help but get upset, not believing I was refused the adoption of a cat and it wasn't even a child! What if the same happened with my application to adopt a child?

I didn't know it at the time but my sister's husband spoke to one of his uncles about the fact that I was desperate for a child. Surprisingly, the uncle proposed himself as a donor and agreed to do that when he got back from his holidays to Morocco in September one month from now. One day before he was due to return back home to France, he suddenly died of a heart attack.

He was only forty seven years old and in good health. I didn't know about this conversation until after his death and I was totally surprised and shocked he even considered and was willing to go ahead with this. What was going on? Was there a message here?

Meanwhile, time for my last treatment was approaching fast and all was going rather well with the medication I was on. Once again Dr Onwude was very hopeful I should get a positive result.

My friend Klara was visiting from the States in September and it was nice to have her company for a few days whilst I was getting my body ready even though I didn't feel like talking much to her about it. At this stage, I needed to focus my energy rather than disperse it. We had fun together as usual, taking long walks by the river and in the park; and I accompanied her at a Kabbalah meeting in Central London. As a Kabbalah member, she strongly believed it was the fast track to spiritual development but she failed to understand each person eventually finds their own, and nothing or no one can force them. Personally, she was pushing too hard to get me to join and instead of helping, it put me off Kabbalah. On one of our evenings out I had to leave the performance of the musical The Lion King to which she invited me to go home and have the last injection I had forgotten. This was so crucial that I didn't care, of course, about missing the show. I came back to the show before it ended to meet her and she didn't notice my absence since we were sitting quite apart thanks to a clerk who got our seating wrong. It worked perfectly.

It was now the 13th October 2008 and here I was once again and for the last time, in Denmark. This time and to everyone's surprise, the clinic aspirated twenty-three follicles and fifteen were of good enough quality to be fertilised. That was it for me now, motherhood or not, life had to move on.

This time, the aspiration left me with some rather uncomfortable cramps in my lower abdomen and I had to take medication to ease the pain. I was focused, calm, at peace and slept a lot. As usual, everyone at the clinic was nice, always wishing me the best after each treatment.

The treatment was now over and I was back home looking after myself and yet again, waiting for the result whichever way it would turn out.

As it happened, of the fifteen follicles sent for fertilization, one and only one fertilised. I was happy at least to have had one egg that could be used.

Some would call it fate, others bad luck but again, it failed. I was now experiencing the biggest disappointment of my life, had absolutely no explanation and could not do anything to change it… it was a total mystery. The only missing part from my life now was the emotional fulfilment within a harmonious family would give me.

I would have to revert back to the conventional way of finding a decent partner if I wished to continue trying for a child. So I brushed disaster aside.

I realised I was going to be watching all my lovely friends go through pregnancy and giving birth to their babies from now on. All I knew was that I needed to be part of their experience and share with them as much as possible. Leaving me out of this would be so much more painful and my closest friends knew this.

I had to come to terms and justify all the expense but I was happy to have done it. At least now I knew I couldn't conceive. I was back on the road to life again on a new adventure but the difference this time was I didn't have a plan anymore. The baby pressure was off my shoulders forever, so I could do whatever I wanted with my life and my savings. Once again, I felt liberated and ever so free. I felt an unexplained security in my life even though my future remained unknown. I had no major worries,

I was healthy and I was going to enjoy every day of the rest of my life.

From the start, my life had been different from many others, seeming I was doing things in reverse order. I was too busy sorting out a career and settling in a home in London before I could think of having a family when I spent ten years with the same partner.

And when I was ready, it just didn't happen. How ironic was that? I didn't need pity either. I had so much peace of mind having tried three times. I also blamed the men in my life for being either too old, too young, smoking or drinking, but of course by choosing them I was confirming to myself what my unconscious mind believed so strongly, perhaps and after all, I really didn't want a family.

In actual fact, I had everything going for me and the fact I didn't succeed in fulfilling a part of my life didn't make me a failure at all. I knew there was much more to life than raising a child.

I was approaching my birthday again, 22nd November 2008 when I would turn forty-six years old. I had dedicated the whole of 2008 to attempting conception and painfully failed. Now I needed to come to terms with it and accept my life as it was. There were so many things I achieved so far and for which I was proud. I had still so much more to do, travelling, writing, singing, doing yoga, dancing, cooking, playing guitar and as long as my energy level allowed I was going to do just that. My plan was to resume travelling again but this time for pleasure only, rather than business.

For my birthday celebration though, I felt I needed my friends around me and organised a lunch in the restaurant of a five star hotel in Central London and to which I only invited my closest friends including David. The day came and I had such a lovely time surrounded by people I loved and cared for and who loved me just for who I was; some of them not even aware of what I had just been through.

It was a long lunch and for mysterious reasons, David failed to turn up at the lunch, which was quite disturbing, but I didn't let it spoil my afternoon. Yet, David turned up shortly after I returned home from lunch that evening, with no explanation other than he forgot about my birthday lunch. The celebration continued until the evening when two of my good neighbours brought a birthday cake to my home with candles and we continued drinking champagne there with David around.

In the meantime, I was getting more and more upset with David and for his lack of consideration for me. I was wondering how I could even put up with such behaviour when I had so much going on. Intimately with him, I experienced something beautifully different and I knew I wanted to find the same in my next relationship. I trusted the Universe would bring to me exactly what I needed when I was ready for it.

That Christmas, I booked myself on a cycling holiday to Cambodia and Vietnam with a circuit covering three hundred and forty kilometres. I was so excited about discovering a new part of the world yet again. Not only was I visiting two new countries but also I was cycling and therefore getting the exercise and the experience of being a lot closer to the locals passing through remote villages.

The trip turned out to be amazing and culturally rich. I felt a great sense of freedom and peace and this meant I could go on with my life. I believed one is the creator of one's life. 2008 was a big year of learning about how I wanted to continue with my life. I wanted to learn new things for as long as I was physically able to do so and wanted to share that feeling with everyone. Even though I wasn't going to experience motherhood, I was still the same person, full of joy, energy and zest for life. After all, I had everything I needed in my life, what else could I wish for?

It was now January 2009 and I needed to put 2008 behind me but my challenges were far from over for me.

Whilst my sister Farida was visiting to celebrate the New Year with me, I received a phone call from my current employer to inform me they couldn't afford to pay my salary anymore which meant as of January 2009, I was officially unemployed.

I couldn't believe it. I was shocked and it was my sister with me who helped me bounce back quickly. She was my guest, and she had come to have fun and relax. I had no time to feel depressed but I still felt deeply betrayed.

After cleaning up a whole database, compiling a training manual and getting new sales, I felt used by my employer who turned out not to be even helpful afterwards. It was a very odd situation with the wife of the owner being constantly there and watching over everything that was happening in the office. Once again, I couldn't understand, I was so trusting of human nature that I couldn't even see when people were using me.

I began to panic and went automatically into survival mode but I was determined since New Year was coming up and Farida was here I wasn't going to let this news spoil my time with her.

This happened on the 30th December 2008 adding the final blow to the year of failures with one failed IUI, three failed IVFs, two failed jobs and a failed relationship. What was I to make of this? What was there for me to learn? I was getting a little tired of all these disappointments and I felt like leaving everything behind and escaping to somewhere nice and warm, which is exactly what happened next.

I celebrated New Year and had a really enjoyable time with my sister. In the next few weeks after she left though, I sat quietly and contemplated my options. Looking for a job, or travelling to do all those things I wanted to do for a long time but couldn't because I was too nervous of not earning a regular salary or missing the opportunity to meet the potential father of my child!

It took me a little while and a lot of courage but I decided to rent out my flat and leave London for a while. It was the best decision I ever made.

Conclusion

It is really difficult to judge what someone else is doing unless you put yourself in their shoes, unless you walk their walk. Everyone comes from different backgrounds, circumstances and life stories.

I'll say it once again. I believe that one is the creator of one's life. 2008 was a big year of learning about what I really wanted, learning so much about myself. I have the feeling I will never stop learning until the day I die which *should be* the story of every human on earth. Even though I wasn't going to experience motherhood, lost jobs and relationships, I was still the same person, full of joy, energy and zest for life.

I am grateful for every new day I experience in my life as I am aware of this process of continued learning and the fact the Universe "has our backs" – and wish to encourage and teach others to be the same.

But most of all, I have found inner peace, the kind already inside each one of us just waiting to find a way out to express itself; the kind all the money in the world could never buy.

After travelling and living in Chile, India, Costa Rica, San Diego and Philadelphia, I decided to settle in Barcelona close enough to my family in Paris and my friends in UK. I am still living there now quite happily, motherless and not married yet at 52 years old.

Also from Oxford eBooks

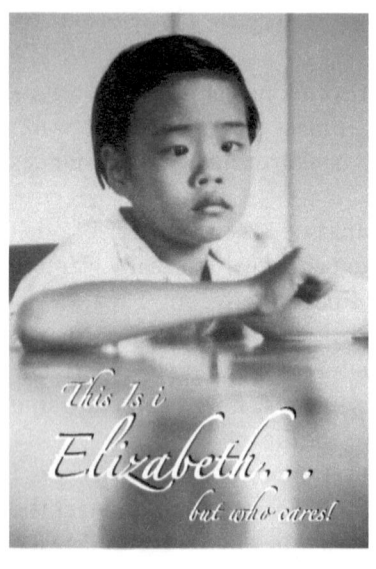

This is I, Elizabeth... but who cares!

When Elizabeth Poey discovered that she had cancer in 2008, her dream of writing a book about her life suddenly became an urgent item on her "To Do" list... and in 2010 when her cancer returned it occupied the number one slot on her "Bucket List".

In this book Elizabeth shares her experiences growing up in Singapore from the 1950's onwards. She records her teenage years and relationships with her extended family, dogs and above all her relationship with God.

Her beautifully recalled story is garnished with many colourful references to life in Singapore, the places, the language, the people... and of course the FOOD. Throughout the book, you will discover photographs of her life and the people closest to her.

As a highly spirited child, she was every teacher's nightmare until she grew up to become a teacher herself. Teacher training days were as fun as they were funny, and she graduated to become a fully trained PE teacher with many wonderful episodes over her 36 year career in education.

The author humbly describes her book as "an autobiography of a nobody", but as you will read, her life has touched and inspired many from her beginnings in a simple Singaporean village to the heights of the Himalayas.

This is I Elizabeth ... but who cares? I know the answer. God does.

Shackled to my Family

Samina Younis

This is the true story of Samina Younis, born in Britain to a strict, religious Muslim family - a family that practices the tradition of forced marriage which they brought back with them from their village in Pakistan.

One of seven sisters and two brothers, she was a bitter disappointment to her parents who desperately wanted a son; as a result she suffered terrible physical and mental abuse at the hands of both her mother and father; later she was to fall victim to continued abuse from her very own siblings.

At the age of just sixteen, on a trip to Pakistan Samina was told that she must marry her second cousin, a boy she had met only once in her life and for whom she had no affection whatsoever.

The writing of this book was Samina's only way of coming to terms with the life that she had been forced into, the mental conflict over her enduring love for a mother, now dead, who even on her deathbed was compelled to dominate and control her future. The book recounts her struggle against her family and her dramatic escape to a life of her own.

www.ingramcontent.com/pod-product-compliance
Lightning Source LLC
Chambersburg PA
CBHW021115080526
44587CB00010B/523